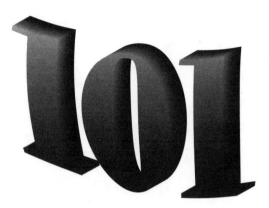

101

WAYS TO MAKE

A TRAINING CTIVE

by
Mel Silberman, Ph.D.
President
Active Training

assisted by
Karen Lawson
President
Lawson Consulting Group

Jossey-Bass
Pfeiffer
San Francisco

Copyright © 1995 by Jossey-Bass/Pfeiffer

ISBN: 0-88390-475-6
Library of Congress Catalog Card Number 95-7738

Library of Congress Cataloging-in-Publication Data

Silberman, Melvin L.

    101 Ways to make training active / by Mel Silberman assisted by Karen Lawson
      p. cm.
    Includes index.
    ISBN 0-88390-475-6 (alk. paper)
    1. Active Learning. 2. Teaching. 3. Adult learning. I. Lawson, Karen. II. Title
    LB1027.23.S55   1995
    371.3—dc20   95-7738

Printed in the United States of America

Published by

350 Sansome Street, 5th Floor
San Francisco, California 94104-1342
(415) 433-1740; Fax (415) 433-0499
(800) 274-4434; Fax (800) 569-0443

Visit our website at: www.pfeiffer.com

Printing 10 9

This book is printed on acid-free, recycled stock that meets or exceeds the minimum GPO and EPA requirements for recycled paper.

CONTENTS

ACKNOWLEDGMENTS

The past five years have been an exhilarating experience for me. Thousands of you have tried active-training techniques and have given me a vote of confidence to keep on developing more. I appreciate the many training professionals, especially fellow chapter members of the American Society for Training and Development, who have engaged in this experimentation and have given me the gift of encouragement and constructive feedback.

I want to thank Sivasailam Thiagarajan, better known as "Thiagi," whose creative ideas have helped me make some of the paradigm shifts necessary for the further development of active-training techniques.

I am also grateful for the contributions of Rebecca Birch and Cynthia Denton-Ade. Rebecca and Cynthia willingly shared with me their active-learning designs that have been a big hit at the conferences of the National Society for Performance and Instruction and graciously agreed to let me include several of the designs in this collection.

Finally, I wish to acknowledge several of my graduate students at Temple University who have assisted me in the creation of active-training ideas. Craig Loundas was particularly helpful in the development of this book. Also, this book would not have been possible without the assistance of Karen Lawson. Thank you.

INTRODUCTION

You can tell people what they need to know very fast.
But, they will forget what you tell them even faster.

People are more likely to understand what they figure out
for themselves than what you figure out for them.

Yes, there is a whole lot more to training than telling! Learning is not an automatic consequence of pouring information into another person's head. It requires the learner's own mental and physical involvement. Lecturing and demonstrating, by themselves, will never lead to real, lasting learning. Only training that is *active* will.

What makes training "active"? When training is active, the participants do most of the work. They use their brains—studying ideas, solving problems, and applying what they learn. Active training is fast-paced, fun, supportive, and personally engaging. Often, participants are out of their seats, moving about and thinking aloud.

Why is it necessary to make training active? In order to learn something well, it helps to hear it, see it, ask questions about it, and discuss it with others. Above all else, we need to "do it." That includes figuring out things by ourselves, coming up with examples, rehearsing skills, and doing tasks that depend on the knowledge we have.

While we know that people learn best by doing, how do we promote active learning in training programs? This sourcebook contains specific, practical strategies that can be used for almost any subject matter. They are designed to enliven your training sessions. Some are a lot of fun and some are downright serious but they all are intended to deepen learning and retention.

101 Ways to Make Training Active brings together in one source a rich, comprehensive collection of training strategies. It is for anyone, experienced or novice, who teaches technical or nontechnical information, concepts, and skills to adults. The book includes ways to get participants active from the start through activities that build teamwork and immediately start people thinking about the subject matter. There are also strategies to conduct full-class learning and small-group learning, to stimulate discussion and debate, to practice skills, to prompt questions, and even to get the participants to teach one another. Finally, there are techniques to review what has been learned, assess how one has changed, and consider the next steps to take so that the training sticks.

The book begins with "The Nuts and Bolts of Active Training." In this part, you will find 160 tips on how to organize and conduct active training. Included are ways to form groups, obtain participation, create classroom layouts, facilitate discussion, and many more suggestions for enhancing the effectiveness of your training efforts.

The 101 special techniques described in this book are divided into three sections:

How to Get Active Participation from the Start

This section contains icebreakers and other kinds of opening activities for any kind of training program. The techniques are designed to do one or more of the following:

- *Team Building:* helping participants to become acquainted with one another or creating a spirit of cooperation and interdependence

- *On-the-Spot Assessment:* learning about the attitudes, knowledge, and experience of participants

- *Immediate Learning Involvement:* creating initial interest in the subject matter

In addition, these techniques encourage participants to take an active role right from the beginning.

How to Teach Information, Skills, and Attitudes Actively

This section contains instructional strategies that can be used when you are at the heart of your training. The techniques are designed either to replace or to reinforce lecture presentations. A wide range of alternatives is provided, all of which gently push participants to think, feel, and apply. The following topics are covered:

- *Full-Class Learning:* trainer-led instruction that stimulates the entire group

- *Stimulating Discussion:* dialogue and debate of key issues

- *Prompting Questions:* participant requests for clarification

- *Team Learning:* tasks done in small groups of participants

- *Peer Teaching:* instruction led by participants

- *Independent Learning:* learning activities performed individually

- *Affective Learning:* activities that help participants to examine their feelings, values, and attitudes

- *Skill Development:* learning and practicing skills, both technical and non-technical

How to Make Training Unforgettable

This section contains ways to conclude a training program so that the participant reflects on what he or she has learned and considers how it will be applied in the future. The focus is not on what you have told the participants, but what they take away. The techniques are designed to address one or more of the following:

- *Reviewing Strategies:* recalling and summarizing what has been learned
- *Self-Assessment:* evaluating changes in knowledge, skills, or attitudes
- *Application Planning:* determining how the learning will be applied by the participant after the training program is over
- *Final Sentiments:* communicating the thoughts, feelings, and concerns participants have at the end

Each of the 101 strategies you are about to read are described and illustrated in the following ways:

- *Overview:* a statement about the purpose of the strategy and the setting in which it is appropriate
- *Procedure:* step-by-step instructions on how to use the strategy
- *Variations:* suggestions for alternative ways to use the strategy

Furthermore, each of the strategies is illustrated by a *Case Example.* These examples are drawn from a wide range of subject matter. The list below summarizes the topical areas you will find illustrated in *101 Ways to Make Training Active:*

AIDS	Cross-Functional Teams
Assertiveness	Customer Service
Benefits	Decision Making
Business Development	Delegation
Business Etiquette	Disabilities
Business Insurance	Diversity
Business Reengineering	Ethics
Business Writing	Facilitation Skills
Career Planning	Group Process
Change Management	Interviewing
Claims	Leadership
Coaching/On-the-Job Training	Math Literacy
Communication	Meetings
Conflict Resolution	Motivation
Creative Problem Solving	New-Employee Orientation

Performance Management Strategic Planning
Presentation Skills Stress Management
Process Improvement Substance Abuse
Product Knowledge Supervisory Skills
Professional Image Team Building
Project Management Telephone Skills
Retirement Planning Time Management
Safety Total Quality Management
Sales Training Techniques
Sexual Harassment

In order to find these examples quickly, use the helpful index at the end of *101 Ways to Make Training Active*.

One final word—use these techniques "as-is" or adapt them to fit your needs. And add your own creativity! As you do, bear in mind these suggestions:

- Don't experiment wildly. Try out a new method no more than once a week.

- When you introduce a method to participants, sell it as an alternative to the usual way of doing things. Obtain their feedback.

- Don't overload participants with too many activities. *Less is often more.* Use just a few to enliven your training program.

- Make your instructions clear. Demonstrate or illustrate what participants are expected to do so that there is no confusion that might distract them from getting the most out of the technique.

The Nuts and Bolts of Active Training

ONE HUNDRED SIXTY TIPS ——————————

In order to facilitate the 101 active training strategies described in this book, you may find it useful to read this section first. Many of the 101 strategies utilize the tips listed here. These tips form the "nuts and bolts" of active training. In my book *Active Training* (Lexington, 1990), I described at length how to design and conduct active, experientially based training programs in private- and public-sector organizations. On the pages that follow, you will find sixteen "top ten" lists, totaling 160 training tips. These lists summarize much of my advice on how to build more quality, activity, variety, and direction into training programs from beginning to end. The lists help trainers identify, at a glance, the top ten choices available to them at different points in the course of doing active training; they will function as useful "building blocks" for the strategies.

Many of the ideas are well known. Having an organized list of them will make your job of being an active trainer easier. Think of these lists as "training menus" from which you might select the option you need at any given moment to make training truly active.

10 Layouts for Setting Up a Training Classroom

The physical environment in a classroom can make or break active training. No setup is ideal but there are many options to choose from. The "interior decorating" of active training is fun and challenging (especially when the furniture is less than ideal). In some cases, furniture can be easily rearranged to create different setups. If you choose to do so, ask participants to help move tables and chairs. That gets them "active" too.

1. **U shape.** This is an all-purpose setup. The participants have a reading and writing surface, they can see you and a visual medium easily, and they are in face-to-face contact with one another. It is also easy to pair up participants, especially when there are two seats per table. The arrangement is ideal for distributing handouts quickly to participants because you can enter the U and walk to different points with sets of materials.

   You can set up oblong tables in a squared-off U:

   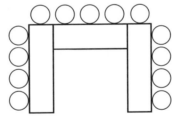

   Be sure there is enough perimeter space in the room so that subgroups of three or more participants can pull back from the tables and face one another.

   When there are more than sixteen participants, a U can start to resemble a bowling alley:

   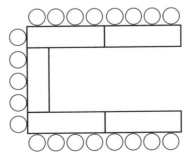

or a bridge:

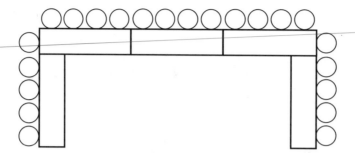

It is much better, in this case, to bring all participants in closer contact by seating some participants inside the U:

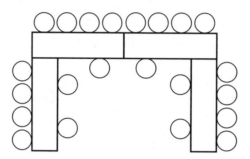

You can also arrange circular or oblong tables in a U that appears more like a semicircle or a horseshoe:

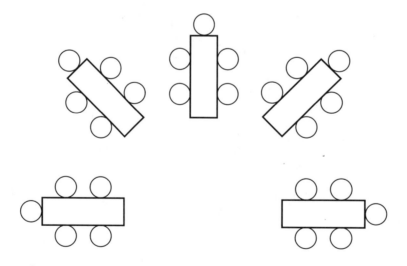

2. Team style. Grouping circular or oblong tables around the room enables you to promote team interaction. You can place seats fully around the tables for the most intimate setting. If you do, some participants will have to turn their chairs around to face the front of the room to see you, a flip chart/blackboard, or a screen.

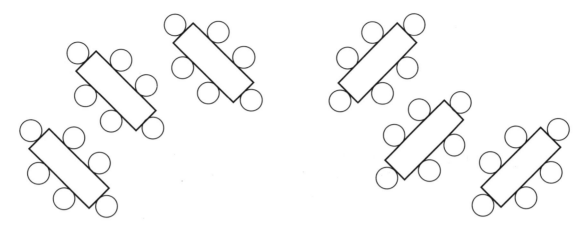

Or you can place seats halfway around the tables so that no participant has his or her back to the front of the room.

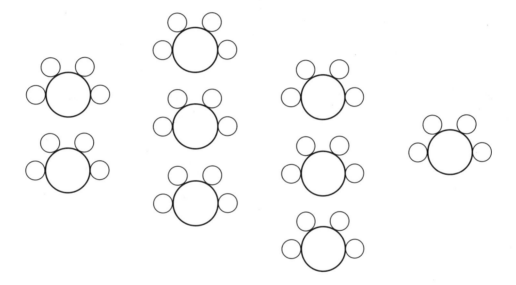

3. **Conference table.** It is best if the table is circular or square. This arrangement minimizes the importance of the leader and maximizes the importance of the group. A rectangular table often creates a sense of formality if the facilitator is at the "head" of the table:

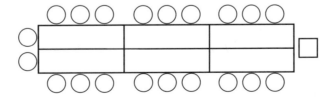

If the facilitator sits in the middle of a wider side of a rectangular table, the participants on the ends will feel left out.

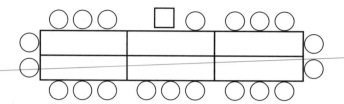

You can form a conference table arrangement by joining together several smaller tables (the center will usually be hollow).

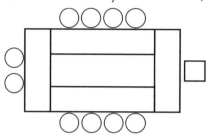

4. **Circle.** Simply seating participants in a circle without tables promotes the most direct face-to-face interaction. A circle is ideal for full-group discussion. Assuming there is enough perimeter space, you can ask participants to quickly arrange their chairs into many subgroup arrangements.

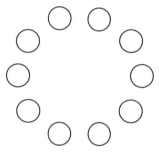

If you want a table surface available for participants, use a peripheral arrangement.

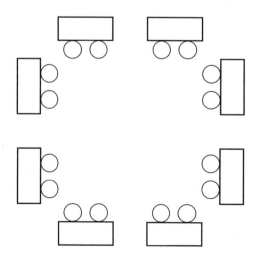

5. Group on group. This arrangement allows you to conduct fishbowl discussions (see "Ten Methods for Obtaining Participation," page 16) and to set up role plays, debates, or observations of group activity. The most typical design is two concentric circles of chairs. Or you can place a meeting table in the middle, surrounded by an outer ring of chairs.

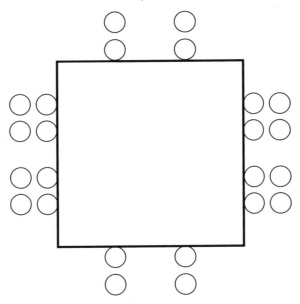

6. Workstations. This arrangement is appropriate for an active, laboratory-type environment in which each participant is seated at a station to perform a procedure or task (for example, using a computer, operating a machine, or drawing) right after it is demonstrated. A terrific way to encourage learning partnerships is to place two participants at the same station. (See "Ten Assignments to Give Learning Partners," page 18.)

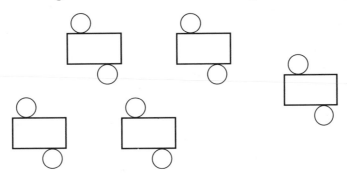

7. Breakout groupings. If the room is large enough or if nearby space is available, arrange (in advance when feasible) tables and/or chairs that subgroups can go to for team-based learning activities. Keep the breakout settings as far from one another as they can be so that each team is not disturbed by the others. However, avoid using breakout spaces that are so far from the room that the connection to it is difficult to maintain.

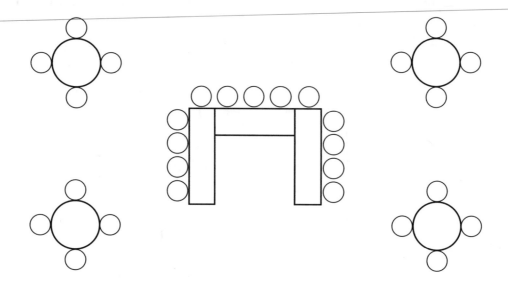

8. Chevron. A traditional classroom setup (rows of desks) does not promote active learning. However, when there are many participants (thirty or more) and only oblong tables are available, it is sometimes necessary to arrange participants "classroom style." A repeated V or chevron arrangement, when possible, creates less distance between people and better frontal visibility. It also provides participants with a greater opportunity to see one another than in the traditional classroom setup. In this arrangement, it is best to place aisles off-center.

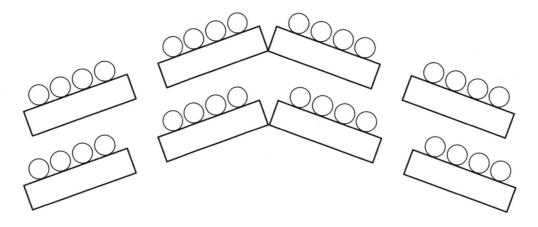

9. Traditional classroom. If you have no choice but to use a series of straight rows of desks/tables and chairs, all is not lost. Group chairs in pairs to allow for the use of learning partners. Try to create an even number of rows and enough space between them so that pairs of participants in the odd-number rows can turn their chairs around and create a quartet with the pair seated directly behind them.

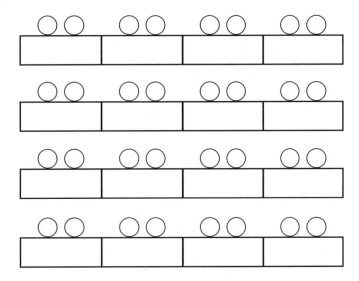

10. **Auditorium.** Although an auditorium is a very limiting environment for active training, there is still hope. If the seats are movable, place them in an arc to create greater closeness and to allow participants to better see one another.

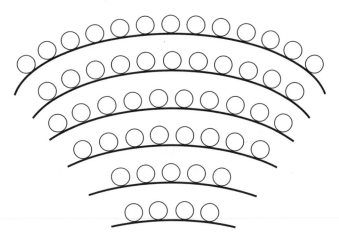

If the seats are fixed, ask participants to seat themselves as close to the center as possible. Be assertive about this request; consider cordoning off sections of the auditorium. *Remember:* No matter how large the auditorium and the size of the audience, you can still pair up participants and use active-training activities that involve learning partners.

10 Techniques for Learning Names

In an active-training environment, the participants are as important as the trainer. When participants are called by their names, they feel important. There are a variety of ways to learn others' names. Some are relatively straightforward; some make learning names into a game.

1. **Name-learning assignment.** Ask participants to learn as many names as possible, either by going up to others and introducing themselves or by reading one anothers' name tags. After several minutes, stop the group and ask the participants to cover up or discard name tags, name lists, and the like. Now, challenge participants to look around and quiz themselves on the names of others in the class. If desired, repeat the learning and self-quizzing activity as many times as you like. Within ten minutes, it should be possible for participants to learn at least twenty names.

2. **Name chain.** Ask each participant in turn to share his or her name and the names of the people who have already introduced themselves. For example, the first person to introduce himself or herself need only say his or her name but the second person is required to give the first person's name as well as his or her own. As the chain becomes longer, there will be more names to remember; however, the names will by then have been repeated several times. You can make the name chain alliterative by inviting each person to use an adjective before his or her name that begins with the same letter, as in "creative Carol" or "lucky Lee." The alliterative adjectives help others to remember the participants' names and often add humor to the activity. Or invite participants to say their names and then accompany them with some physical movement. The movement then becomes a mnemonic aid.

3. **Alphabetical lineup.** Invite participants to arrange themselves in alphabetical order by their first names. This task forces participants to find out other names in the group. Or do a "nonverbal name lineup" as a way to review names after participants have introduced themselves in conventional fashion. Ask participants to line up in alphabetical order by their first names *without talking to each other.*

4. **Name bingo.** Ask participants to mill around the room and meet one another. As they exchange names, have them write each name anywhere on a blank bingo form you have made for them. Create a 3 x 3 format of squares if the group has fewer than ten people, a 4 x 4 format if the group has sixteen or fewer and a 5 x 5 format if the group has twenty-five or fewer. Instruct participants to place an "O" on any box not used up after meeting each participant. Then place a copy of everyone's name in a hat. As the hat is passed around the group, each participant picks a name out of the hat. Everyone places an "X" on the box on their form containing the name picked. Whenever any player obtains bingo (horizontally, vertically, or diagonally), he or she yells "Bingo!" Eventually, everyone will get bingo several times.

5. **Name tag mix-up.** Give each participant the name tag of someone else in the group and ask each person to find the owner of the name tag. Invite participants to circulate until every person receives his or her name tag.

6. **Alphabetical sign-in.** Premark sheets of flip-chart paper with the letters of the alphabet. Tape the flip-chart paper to walls around the room. Direct participants to sign the sheet containing the first initial of their name and to find others with the same initial. Then instruct the participants to look over the other sheets and attempt to identify as many names and faces as possible.

7. **Do you know your neighbors?** Form a circle and place one participant in the middle. Ask that person to point to someone in the circle and challenge him or her with the question "Do you know your neighbors?" If the person in the circle can successfully say the name of the people immediately to his or her right and left, the person in the middle stays there and challenges another person in the circle. When a participant fails the neighbor test, he or she replaces the person in the middle. As the game is played, frequently change the positions of the participants in the circle.

8. **Personalized name tags.** Provide materials so that each participant can develop a name tag that uses any of the following:

   - interesting calligraphy
   - a personal logo
   - a zodiac sign
   - an object or animal that symbolizes some personal quality
   - a coat of arms
   - a collage of magazine cutouts that contain favorite expressions or objects

Ask participants to meet one another and to learn names.

9. **Name toss.** Have group members stand in a circle with one person holding an object that can be easily thrown and caught, such as a ball or a beanbag. The member holding the object says his or her name and tosses the object to another group member. The person catching the object gives his or her name and tosses the object to another group member. Continue the tossing until all participants have introduced themselves. When the final member has been introduced, ask that person to say the name of another group member and then toss the object to that person. The receiver than repeats the name of the person who tossed him or her the object and says the name of another group member before tossing the object to that person.

10. **What's in a name?** Have participants introduce themselves and then share any of the following about their names:

   - what I like or dislike about my name
   - who I was named after
   - a nickname that I like or dislike
   - the origin of my name

   After these introductions, challenge participants to write down the names of all the members of the group.

10 Questions for Obtaining Participant Expectations

There are a variety of questions you can ask to find out the needs, expectations, and concerns of the participants so that you can gear instruction appropriately. You can obtain answers through open discussion, a whip, response cards, fishbowls, polling, panels, games, and so on. (See "Ten Methods for Obtaining Participation," page 16.)

1. Why did you choose this class? Why did you come?

2. What questions about [subject matter of class] do you come with?

3. What advice, information, or skills do you want to get from this class?

4. What advice, information, or skills don't you need or don't you want?

5. What do you want to take away from this class? Name one thing.

6. What are your hopes for this class? What are your concerns?

7. Do the class objectives match your needs?

8. What knowledge or skills do you feel you "need" to have? What would be "nice" to have?

9. What are your expectations about this class?

10. What have you learned from previous classes on this topic?

10 Methods for Obtaining Participation

Active training cannot occur without the involvement of participants. There are a variety of ways to structure discussion and to obtain responses from participants during a session. Some methods are especially suitable when time is limited or participation needs to be coaxed. You might also consider combining these methods. For example, you might use subgroup discussion and then invite a spokesperson from each subgroup to serve on a panel.

1. **Open discussion.** Address an unstructured question to the entire group. The straightforward quality of open discussion is appealing. If you are worried that the discussion might be too lengthy, say beforehand, "I'd like to ask four or five participants to share...." To encourage participants to raise their hands, ask, "How many of you have a response to my question?" Then call on one of the hands that are raised.

2. **Response cards.** Pass out index cards and request anonymous answers to your questions. Use response cards to save time or to provide anonymity for personally threatening self-disclosures. The need to state yourself concisely on a card is another advantage of this method. (See "Ten Occasions to Use Response Cards," page 19.)

3. **Polling.** Design a short survey that is filled out and tallied on the spot, or verbally poll participants. Use polling to obtain data quickly and in a quantifiable form. If you use a written survey, try to supply the results to participants as quickly as possible. If you use a verbal survey, ask for a show of hands or invite participants to hold up answer cards. (See strategy 14, "Instant Assessment," page 73.)

4. **Subgroup discussion.** Form participants into subgroups of three or more to share and record information. Use subgroup discussion when you have sufficient time to process questions and issues. This is one of the key methods for obtaining everyone's participation. (See "Ten Strategies for Forming Groups," page 23.)

5. **Learning partners.** Form participants into pairs and instruct them to work on tasks or discuss key questions. Use learning partners when you

want to involve everybody but do not have enough time for small-group discussion. A pair is a good group configuration for developing a supportive relationship and/or for working on complex activities that would not lend themselves to large-group configurations. (See "Ten Assignments to Give Learning Partners," page 18.)

6. **Whips.** Ask each participant for a short response to a key question. Use whips when you want to obtain something quickly from each participant. Sentence stems (for example, "One thing that makes a manager effective...") are useful in conducting whips. Invite participants to pass when they wish. Avoid repetition, if you want, by asking each participant for a new contribution to the process.

7. **Panels.** Invite a small number of participants to present their views in front of the entire class. An informal panel can be created by asking for the views of a designated number of participants who remain in their seats. Use panels when time permits to generate focused, serious responses to your questions. Rotate panelists to increase participation.

8. **Fishbowl.** Ask a portion of the group to form a discussion circle and have the remaining participants form a listening circle around them. Rotate new groups into the inner circle to continue the discussion. (See strategy 36, "Three-Stage Fishbowl Discussion," page 130.) Use fishbowl discussions to help bring focus to large-group discussions. Although time consuming, this is the best method for combining the virtues of large- and small-group discussion. As a variation to concentric circles, participants can remain seated at tables and you can invite different tables or parts of a table to discuss the topic as the others listen.

9. **Games.** Use an enjoyable activity or a quiz game to elicit participants' ideas, knowledge, or skills. Use games to stimulate energy and involvement. Games also help to make dramatic points that participants seldom forget.

10. **Calling on the next speaker.** Ask participants to raise their hands when they want to share their views and request that the present speaker call on the next speaker (rather than the instructor performing this role). Use this method when you are sure there is a lot of interest in the discussion or activity and you wish to promote participant interaction.

10 Assignments to Give Learning Partners

One of the most effective and efficient ways to promote active training is to divide a class into pairs and compose learning partnerships. It is hard to get left out in a pair. It is also hard to hide in one. Learning partnerships can be short term or long term. Learning partners can undertake a wide variety of quick tasks or more time-consuming assignments, such as those in the list below.

1. **Read,** critique, or edit each other's written work.

2. **Interview** each other concerning reactions to an assigned reading or a video.

3. **Read** and discuss a short written document with each other.

4. **Question** each other about an assigned reading.

5. **Recap** a lecture or demonstration with each other.

6. **Develop** questions together to ask the facilitator.

7. **Analyze** a case problem, exercise, or experiment together.

8. **Test** each other.

9. **Respond** to a question posed by the facilitator.

10. **Compare** notes taken in class.

10 Occasions to Use Response Cards

One of the simplest ways to engender thought and discussion is to ask participants to write a response on a blank index card. These cards, once written on, can be kept by the writer to ponder and to stimulate contributions to class-wide discussion. Or the cards can be collected, shuffled, and distributed to participants (each of whom then receives a card whose author is unknown). Finally, the cards can be passed around a group so that each participant can read what others have written. There are many things you can ask participants to write on their response cards.

1. **A question** about the subject matter of the session.

   What do you think the "platinum rule" is?

2. **An answer** to a test question posed by the trainer.

   Force-field analysis is a problem-solving technique.

3. **An expectation** or need each participant has about the session.

   I want to learn how to accommodate workers with disabilities.

4. **A solution** to a case problem.

   One way that Mr. Brown can reduce his tax burden is by purchasing tax-deferred annuities.

5. **A definition** for an important term.

   Sexual harassment means unwelcome sexual advances, requests for sexual favors, or remarks that interfere with the performance of one's job.

6. **A belief** or opinion held by the participant.

   A diverse workforce has more benefits than drawbacks.

7. **A fact** about the subject matter that the participant believes to be true.

   The AIDS virus has a long latency period.

8. **A hypothesis** about an experiment or research project.

   Males over six feet tall are more likely to obtain advancement than those who are under six feet tall.

9. **A preference** held by the participant.

   I dislike role playing.

10. **A proverb,** slogan, or title (book, movie, song, etc.) that the participant favors.

   Just do it!

10 Suggestions for Improving a Lecture

Lecturing is one of the most time-honored yet ineffective ways to teach. By itself, it will never lead to active learning. For a lecture to be effective, the trainer should build interest first, then maximize understanding and retention, involve participants during the lecture, and reinforce what has been presented. There are several ways to do just that.

Building Interest

1. **Lead-off story or interesting visual.** Provide a relevant anecdote, fictional story, cartoon, or graphic that captures the audience's attention.

2. **Initial case problem.** Present a problem around which the lecture will be structured.

3. **Test question.** Ask participants a question (even if they have little prior knowledge) so that they will be motivated to listen to your lecture for the answer.

Maximizing Understanding and Retention

4. **Headlines.** Reduce the major points in the lecture to key words that act as verbal subheadings or memory aids.

5. **Examples and analogies.** Provide real-life illustrations of the ideas in the lecture and, if possible, create a comparison between your material and the knowledge and experience that the participants already have.

6. **Visual backup.** Use flip charts, transparencies, brief handouts, and demonstrations that enable participants to see as well as hear what you are saying.

Involving Participants During the Lecture

7. **Spot challenges.** Interrupt the lecture periodically and challenge participants to give examples of the concepts presented thus far or to answer spot quiz questions.

8. Illuminating activities. Throughout the presentation, intersperse brief activities that illuminate the points you are making.

Reinforcing the Lecture

9. Application problem. Pose a problem or question for participants to solve based on the information given in the lecture.

10. Participant review. Ask participants to review the contents of the lecture with one another or give them a self-scoring review test.

10 Strategies for Forming Groups

Small-group work is an important part of active training. It is important to form groups quickly and efficiently and, at the same time, to vary the composition and sometimes the size of the groups throughout the session. The following options are interesting alternatives to letting participants choose their own groups or counting off up to a designated number.

1. **Grouping cards.** Determine how many participants will be attending the session and how many different groupings you want throughout the session. For example, in a class of twenty, one activity may call for four groups of five; another, five groups of four; still another, six groups of three with two observers.

   Code these groups using a colored dot (red, blue, green, and yellow for four groups), decorative stickers (different stickers in a common theme for five groups, such as lions, monkeys, tigers, giraffes, and elephants), and a number (1 through 6 for six groups). Randomly place a number, a colored dot, and a sticker on a card for each participant and include the card in the participant's materials. When you are ready to form your groups, identify which code you are using and direct the participants to join their groups in a designated place. Participants will be able to move quickly to their groups, saving time and eliminating confusion. You may want to post signs indicating group meeting areas to make the process even more efficient.

2. **Puzzles.** Purchase six-piece children's jigsaw puzzles or create your own by cutting out pictures from magazines, pasting them on cardboard, and cutting them into your desired shape, size, and number of pieces. Select the number of puzzles according to the number of groups you want to create. Separate the puzzles, mix up the pieces, and give each participant a puzzle piece. When you are ready to form the participants into groups, instruct the participants to locate others with the pieces to complete a puzzle.

3. **Finding famous fictional friends and families.** Create a list of famous fictional family members or friends in groups of three or four. (Examples are Peter Pan, Tinkerbell, Captain Hook, Wendy; Alice, Cheshire Cat,

Queen of Hearts, Mad Hatter; Superman, Lois Lane, Jimmy Olsen, Clark Kent.) Choose the same number of fictional characters as there are participants. Write one fictional name on each index card. Shuffle or mix up the cards and give each participant a card. When you are ready to form groups, ask the participants to find the other members of their "family." Once the famous group is complete, they are to find a spot to congregate.

4. **Name tags.** Use name tags of different shapes and/or colors to designate different groupings.

5. **Birthdays.** Ask participants to line up by birthdays and then break into the number of subgroups needed for a particular activity. In large groups, form subgroups by birth months. For example, 150 participants can be divided into three roughly equal-size groups by composing groups of those born in January, February, March, and April; May, June, July, and August; and September, October, November, and December.

6. **Playing cards.** Use a deck of playing cards to designate groups. For example, use jacks, queens, kings, and aces to create four groups of four. Use additional number cards, if necessary, to accommodate a larger group. Shuffle the cards and deal one to each participant. Then direct the participants to locate others with similar cards and to form a group.

7. **Draw numbers.** Determine the number and size of the groups you want to create, put numbers on individual slips of paper, and place them in a box. Participants then draw a number from the box indicating which group number they belong to. For example, if you want four groups of four, you would have sixteen slips of paper with four each of the numbers 1 through 4.

8. **Candy flavors.** Give each participant a wrapped sugarless candy of a different flavor to indicate groups. For example, your groups may be categorized as lemon, butterscotch, cherry, and mint.

9. **Choose like items.** Select toys of a common theme to indicate groups. For example, you might choose transportation and use cars, airplanes, boats, and trains. Each participant would draw a toy from a box and locate others with the same toy to form a group.

10. **Participant materials.** You can code participant materials using colored paper clips, colored handouts, or stickers on folders or tent cards to predetermine groupings.

10 Alternatives for Selecting Group Leaders and Filling Other Jobs

One of the ways to facilitate active learning in small groups is to assign jobs such as leader, facilitator, timekeeper, recorder, spokesperson, process observer, or materials manager to some of the group members. Often, you can ask for volunteers to assume some of these responsibilities. Sometimes, it is fun and efficient to use a creative selection strategy.

1. **Alphabetical assignment.** Assign jobs in alphabetical order by first name. In a long-term group, rotate jobs using this order.

2. **Birthday assignment.** Make assignments in chronological order by participants' birthdays. In a long-term group, rotate jobs using this order.

3. **Number lottery.** Ask group members to count off. Place pieces of paper with the numbers held by group members in a hat, draw a number, and assign the person with that number to the job.

4. **Color lottery.** Select a color for each assignment. The person who is wearing that color receives that assignment.

5. **Article of clothing.** Assign responsibilities by selecting corresponding articles of clothing such as eyeglasses, silver jewelry, a sweater, or brown shoes.

6. **Voting.** Ask group members to vote on the job recipient. One popular method (used by Bob Pike[1]) is to signal members to point to the person they are voting for. The person with the most fingers pointing at him or her gets the job.

7. **Random assignment.** Ask each member to reveal the sum of the last four digits of his or her home phone number (for example, 9999 equals thirty-six). Announce a number from one to thirty-six. Award the job to the person in the group whose sum comes closest to that number.

---

[1] Robert Pike, President, Creative Training Techonolgies International, Edina, MN.

8. **Pet lovers.** Assign a designated job to the person with the greatest number of pets.

9. **Family size.** Assign a designated job to the person with the most (or fewest) siblings.

10. **Door prize.** Prior to the session, place a sticker in such a way as to identity one member per group. You might place a sticker on a name tag, on a seat or desk, or on one of the instructional handouts. The person receiving the sticker gets the prize of a specific group job. For awarding more than one job, use stickers of different colors.

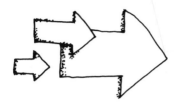

10 Tips When Facilitating Discussion

Your role during a group discussion is to facilitate the flow of comments from participants. Although it is not necessary to interject your comments after each participant speaks, periodically assisting the group with their contributions can be helpful. Here is a ten-point facilitation menu to use as you lead group discussions.

1. **Paraphrase** what a participant has said so that he or she feels understood and so that the other participants can hear a concise summary of what has been said.

   So, what you're saying is that you have to be very careful about asking applicants where they live during an interview because it might suggest some type of racial or ethnic affiliation. You also told us that it's okay to ask for an interviewee's address on a company application form.

2. **Check** your understanding of a participant's statement or ask the participant to clarify what he or she is saying.

   Are you saying that this plan is not realistic? I'm not sure that I understand exactly what you meant. Could you please run it by us again?

3. **Compliment** an interesting or insightful comment.

   That's a good point. I'm glad that you brought that to our attention.

4. **Elaborate** on a participant's contribution to the discussion with examples, or suggest a new way to view the problem.

   Your comments provide an interesting point from the employee's perspective. It could also be useful to consider how a manager would view the same situation.

5. **Energize** a discussion by quickening the pace, using humor, or, if necessary, prodding the group for more contributions.

   Oh my, we have lots of humble people in this group! Here's a challenge for you. For the next two minutes, let's see how many ways you can think of to increase cooperation within your department.

6. **Disagree** (gently) with a participant's comments to stimulate further discussion.

I can see where you are coming from, but I'm not sure that what you are describing is always the case. Has anyone else had an experience that is different from Jim's?

7. **Mediate** differences of opinion between participants and relieve any tensions that may be brewing.

I think that Susan and Mary are not really disagreeing with each other but are just bringing out two different sides of this issue.

8. **Pull together** ideas, showing their relationship to each other.

As you can see from Dan's and Jean's comments, personal goal setting is very much a part of time management. You need to be able to establish goals for yourself on a daily basis in order to more effectively manage your time.

9. **Change** the group process by altering the method for obtaining participation or by having the group evaluate ideas that have been presented.

Let's break into smaller groups and see if you can come up with some typical customer objections to the products that were covered in the presentation this morning.

10. **Summarize** (and record, if desired) the major views of the group.

I have noted four major reasons that have come from our discussion as to why managers do not delegate: (1) lack of confidence, (2) fear of failure, (3) comfort in doing the task themselves, and (4) fear of being replaced.

10 Options for Role Playing

Role playing is one of the most useful methods to explore attitudes and to practice skills. To be successful when conducting a role play, it helps to know different ways to set it up (scripting) and to lead it (formatting).

Scripting

1. **Free form.** Give participants a general scenario and ask them to fill in the details themselves.

2. **Prescribed.** Give participants a well-prepared set of instructions that state the facts about the roles they are portraying and how they are to behave.

3. **Partially prescribed.** Give participants extensive background information about the situation and the characters to be portrayed but do not tell them how to handle the situation.

4. **Replay life.** Ask participants to reenact an actual situation that they have faced.

5. **Dramatic reading.** Give participants a previously prepared script to act out.

Formatting

6. **Simultaneous.** Form all participants into subgroups of appropriate sizes (for example, pairs for a two-person drama, trios for a three-person drama) and have all groups simultaneously undertake their role plays.

7. **Stage front.** Have one or more participants role play in front of the group. Ask the rest of the participants to observe and provide feedback.

8. **Rotational.** Rotate the participants in front of the group by interrupting the role play in progress and substituting a new participant for one or more of the role players.

9. **Different actors.** Recruit more than one participant to role play the same situation. This allows the group to observe more than one style.

10. **Repeated.** Practice the role play a second time.

10 Steps to Use When Facilitating Experiential Activities

Experiential activities really help to make training active. It is often far better for participants to experience something rather than to hear it talked about. Such activities typically involve role playing, games, simulations, visualization, and problem-solving tasks. The following ten steps will help to make your experiential activities a success.

1. **Explain your objectives.** Participants like to know what is going to happen and why.

2. **Sell the benefits.** Explain why you are doing the activity and how the activity connects with any preceding activities.

3. **Speak slowly when giving directions.** You might also provide visual backup. Make sure the instructions are understood.

4. **Demonstrate the activity if the directions are complicated.** Let the participants see the activity in action before they do it.

5. **Divide participants into the subgroups before giving further directions.** If you do not, participants may forget the instructions while the subgroups are being formed.

6. **Inform participants how much time they have.** State the time you have allotted for the entire activity and then periodically announce how much time remains.

7. **Keep the activity moving.** Don't slow things down by endlessly recording participant contributions on flip charts or blackboards and don't let a discussion drag on for too long.

8. **Challenge the participants.** More energy is created when activities generate a moderate level of tension. If tasks are a snap, participants will get lethargic.

9. **Always discuss the activity.** When an activity has concluded, invite participants to process their feelings and to share their insights and learnings.

10. **Structure the first processing experiences.** Guide the discussion carefully and ask questions that will lead to participant involvement and input. If participants are in subgroups, ask each person to take a brief turn sharing his or her responses.

10 Timesavers When Active Training Takes Time

Active training takes time. Therefore, it is crucial that no time is wasted. The following are some ways to avoid wasting time.

1. **Start on time.** This act sends a message to latecomers that you are serious. If all of the participants are not yet in the room, begin the session, if you wish, with a discussion or filler activity for which complete attendance is not necessary.

2. **Give clear instructions.** Do not start an activity when participants are confused about what to do. If the directions are complicated, put them in writing.

3. **Prepare visual information ahead of time.** Do not write lecture points on flip charts or a blackboard while participants watch. Have the notes prerecorded. Also, decide if recording participant input is really necessary. If so, don't record the discussion verbatim. Use "headlines" to capture what participants are saying.

4. **Distribute handouts quickly.** Prepare handouts in stapled packets prior to the session. Distribute packets to key areas of the room so that several people can assist with distribution.

5. **Expedite subgroup reporting.** Ask subgroups to list their ideas on flip-chart paper and to post their lists on the walls of the room so that all the work can be viewed and discussed at the same time. Or, going from group to group, have each group report only one item at a time so that everyone can listen for possible overlap. Subgroups should not repeat what has already been said.

6. **Do not let discussions be too long.** Express the need to move on, but be sure in a later discussion to call on those who didn't have a chance to contribute previously. Or begin a discussion by stating a time limit and suggesting how many contributions time will permit.

7. **Obtain volunteers swiftly.** Don't wait endlessly for participants to volunteer. You can recruit volunteers during breaks in the session. Continue to call on individual participants if there are no immediate volunteers. Or use any of the methods in "Ten Alternatives for Selecting Group Leaders and Filling Other Jobs," page 25.

8. **Be prepared for tired or lethargic groups.** Provide a list of ideas, questions, or even answers and ask participants to select ones they agree with; frequently, your list will trigger thoughts and issues from participants.

9. **Quicken the pace of activities from time to time.** Often, setting time limits for participants energizes them and makes them more productive.

10. **Elicit prompt attention.** Use a variety of cues or attention-getting devices to inform the participants that you are ready to reconvene after a small-group activity. (See "Ten Tricks for Calling Participants to Order," page 35.)

10 Tricks for Calling Participants to Order

When training is active, the room can become busy with activity and even noisy. From time to time, you will need to get the attention of participants to indicate that a time period is up and that you will be leading the group into a new phase. There are several ways to accomplish this.

1. **Flick a light switch.** This isn't offensive if you do it rapidly and briefly.

2. **Make a dramatic announcement.** Grab attention by saying something like "Testing, 1, 2, 3. Testing," "Now hear this, now hear this," or "Earth to group, earth to group." Use a megaphone or microphone for large groups.

3. **Create a verbal wave.** Instruct the group to repeat after you whenever they hear you say "time's up." In no time at all, the participants will be assisting you in indicating that it is time to stop what they are doing.

4. **Use clapping.** Instruct the group members to clap their hands once if they can hear you. Within a few seconds, the first participants to hear your instructions will clap and by doing so, will get the rest of the group's attention.

5. **Play prerecorded music.** Select music that can quickly command attention. You may elect to quiet participants gently, using meditative music, or with a bang, using something like the opening bar of Beethoven's Fifth.

6. **Use a silent signal.** Explain to participants that they should quiet down whenever they see you using a particular signal (for example, holding up your index and middle fingers). Encourage the participants to do the signal as well.

7. **Use a sound signal.** A gavel, bell, whistle, or kazoo will do. Novelty stores also have a variety of sound-making gag toys.

8. **Tell a joke.** Inform participants that you have a storehouse of jokes or riddles that will serve as a cue to quiet down.

9. **"Can we talk?"** Use Joan Rivers' famous line as a way to reconvene the entire group for discussion.

10. **Announce "break-time!"** This will surely get everyone's attention.

10 Props That Dramatize Learning

Props are an excellent way to create interest through visual impact and to promote learning retention. Use your imagination to select objects such as hats, pictures, toys, or signs to illustrate your point and enhance your presentation.

1. **Train whistle.** Use a train signal to alert participants to finish up a subgroup activity or to start another. What could be a more appropriate way to let them know that this "train"-ing is coming in on time?

2. **Picture perfect.** Peruse magazines and catalogs for pictures relating to your topic and use them to test assumptions, illustrate a point, or spark a discussion. For example, in a session on diversity, choose pictures of people of different ages, genders, races, or ethnic backgrounds shown in a variety of settings and ask participants to guess the occupation of each person and to give the reasons for their answers. This is an interesting way to begin to examine stereotypes and assumptions.

3. **Abracadabra.** Use a magic wand or a crystal ball to introduce the topic of management-skills by pointing out that many people are promoted to management positions with little or no training and "like magic" are expected to know how to manage. In a session on career development, you can point out that many people expect their careers to happen "like magic" and stress how important it is to take control and to develop a plan instead.

4. **Take one.** Make or buy a film director's clapboard to use in role plays when you want to stop the action to coach the participants or to have the group give feedback on the role play.

5. **Toys R Us.** Simple children's toys can be used in a variety of ways. For example, select a number of different toys based on the number of participants in your session. Possible choices include Silly Putty®, a yo-yo, a Slinky®, a Koosh®ball, or a puzzle. Ask participants to choose a toy and then have them explain how this represents their organization, themselves, or the topic. You can also use toys in a sales training session by

asking participants to describe the features and benefits of the toy or to try to "sell" the toy to the rest of the class. Toys can also be used to make a break more enjoyable.

6. **Hat in hand.** Use hats in role plays to help the participants "get into" their roles. For example, have a manager-coach wear a baseball cap. In team building, team hats with logos help create a sense of unity and team spirit.

7. **Post it.** Create posters with quotations from famous people that relate to the topic of the session and display the posters around the room. Not only do they help create a mood and generate interest, but you can also use them to begin the session by asking participants to choose the quotation that they like the best and to explain how they think it relates to the session.

8. **Personification.** Dress up in a costume relating to the subject of the session. For example, in a nursing class on dealing with geriatric patients, you could dress as an old woman or man who has to be helped into the room. To introduce a session on the Americans with Disabilities Act, you can enter the room in a wheelchair or on crutches and discuss with participants how they react to people with disabilities. You could also have participants simulate what it is like to be disabled by using ear plugs to approximate hearing loss, putting petroleum jelly on a pair of glasses to simulate the loss of sight, or tying a person's arm down to represent the loss of a limb.

9. **Good answer.** Write on a card in large letters, "Good Answer." Give the card to a person in the front of the room. During the discussion, when a participant responds with a good answer to a question, point to the person who has the card who will then hold up the "Good Answer" card for all to see.

10. **Team theme.** Choose a theme for your session. It can relate to an upcoming holiday, a metaphor for the topic, or an organization's theme. Then decorate the room and choose various props that illustrate the theme. For example, a metaphor for team building could be a cruise. When participants arrive, they are greeted with leis and given compasses to help them "stay on course." You could also give them a roll of LifeSaver® candies for that needed "pick-me-up" in the afternoon.

10 Interventions for Regaining Control of the Group

Using active-training techniques tends to minimize the problems that often plague trainers who rely too heavily on lecture and full-group discussion. Nonetheless, difficulties such as monopolizing, distracting, and withdrawing still may occur. Below are interventions you can use; some work well with individual participants while others work with the entire group.

1. **Signal nonverbally.** Make eye contact with or move closer to participants when they hold private conversations, start to fall asleep, or hide from participation. Press your fingers together to signal for a wordy participant to finish what he or she is saying. Make a "T" sign with your fingers to stop unwanted behavior.

2. **Listen actively.** When participants monopolize discussion, go off on a tangent, or argue with you, interject with a summary of their views and then ask others to speak. Or acknowledge the value of their viewpoints and invite them to discuss their views with you during a break.

3. **Encourage new volunteers.** When a few participants repeatedly speak up in class while others hold back, pose a question or problem and then ask how many people have a response to it. You should see new hands go up. Call on one of them. The same technique might work when trying to obtain volunteers for role playing.

4. **Invoke participation rules.** From time to time, tell participants that you would like to use rules such as the following:

   - No one may laugh during a role play.

   - Only participants who have not yet spoken can participate.

   - Each new comment must build on a previous idea.

   - Speak for yourself, not for others.

5. **Use good-natured humor.** One way to deflect difficult behavior is to use humor. Be careful, however, not to be sarcastic or patronizing. Gently protest the inappropriate behavior ("Enough, enough for one day!") or

humorously put yourself down instead of the participant ("I guess I'm being stubborn, but...").

6. **Connect on a personal level.** Even if the problem participants are hostile or withdrawn, make a point of getting to know them during breaks or lunch. It is unlikely that people will continue to give you a hard time or remain distant if you have taken an interest in them.

7. **Change the method of participation.** Sometimes, you can control the damage done by difficult participants by inserting new formats, such as using pairs or small groups rather than full-class activities.

8. **Ignore mildly negative behaviors.** Try to pay little or no attention to behaviors that are small nuisances. These behaviors may disappear if you simply continue the session.

9. **Discuss very negative behaviors in private.** You must call a stop to behaviors that you find detrimental to the training session. Arrange a break and firmly request, in private, a change in behavior of those participants who are disruptive. Or create small-group activities and call aside the problem participants. If the entire group is involved, stop the session and explain clearly what you need from participants to conduct the training effectively.

10. **Do not take personally the difficulties you encounter.** Remember that many problem behaviors have nothing to do with you. Instead, they are due to personal fears and needs or displaced anger. Try to determine if this is the case and ask whether participants can put aside the conditions affecting their positive involvement in the training session.

*H*ow to Get Active Participation from the Start

TEAM-BUILDING STRATEGIES

The strategies that follow are ways to help participants to get acquainted and reacquainted or to build team spirit with an intact group. They also promote an active-learning environment by getting participants to move physically, to share openly their opinions and feelings, and to accomplish something in which they can take pride. Many of these strategies are well known throughout the training profession. Some are my own original creations. All of them get participants active from the start.

When you use these team-building strategies, try to relate them to the subject matter of your training session. Also, experiment with strategies new to you and your participants. In today's world, training participants are so accustomed to certain popular icebreakers that they may be turned off by them rather than turned on. Participants will welcome activities that are refreshingly different.

1 **Trading Places**

```
┌─────────────────── Overview ───────────────────┐
│                                                 │
│  This technique allows participants to get acquainted; │
│  exchange opinions; and consider new ideas, values, or │
│  solutions to problems. It is a great way to promote │
│  self-disclosure or an active exchange of viewpoints. │
│                                                 │
└─────────────────────────────────────────────────┘
```

Procedure

1. Give participants one or more Post-it™ notes. (Decide whether the activity will work better by limiting the participants to one contribution or several.)

2. Ask the participants to write on their note(s) one of the following:

   - a value they hold
   ✓ ■ a recent experience
   - a creative idea or solution to a problem you have posed ✓
   - a question about the subject matter of the training program ✓
   - an opinion about a topic of your choosing
   - a fact about themselves or the subject matter of the session

3. Ask participants to stick the note(s) on their clothing and to circulate around the room reading one another's notes.

4. Next, have participants mingle once again and negotiate trades for other notes. The trades should be based on a desire to possess that value, experience, idea, question, opinion, or fact for a short period of time. Require that all trades be two-way. Encourage participants to make as many trades as they would like.

5. Reconvene the full group and ask participants to share what trades they made and why. For example, "I traded for a note that Sally had, stating that she has traveled to Eastern Europe. I would really like to travel there because my ancestors are from Hungary and Ukraine."

Variations

1. Ask participants to form subgroups rather than trade notes and have them discuss the contents of their notes.

2. Have participants post their notes in a public display (on a blackboard or flip chart) and discuss similarities and differences.

Case Example

This activity is appropriate for a workshop on cultural diversity. It is designed to help a diverse group of participants become acquainted and to promote self-disclosure.

1. Introduce the activity by discussing how our society rewards conformity and minimizes, even ignores, diversity. Indicate, however, that in this activity, individuality is valued.

2. Give each participant six Post-it notes or stick-on notes. Ask participants to write on each a label that might distinguish them from some or all of the other participants. Examples of categories include gender, ethnicity, race, age, physical characteristics, sexual orientation, religion, place of birth, educational level, language differences, economic status, and birth order.

3. Have participants stick their notes on their clothing and then instruct them to stand up and mingle, "hawking" their unique qualities.

4. After a while, invite participants to trade notes with one another. Insist that the trades be two-way and that the participants assume their new identities temporarily. For example, a male participant might trade his "gender" with a female participant.

5. Reconvene the full group and ask for volunteers to share some of the trades they made and why they did so.

2 **Human Scavenger Hunt**

┌─────────────────── **Overview** ───────────────────┐

This is a popular icebreaker that can be designed in a
number of ways and for any size of group. It fosters team
building and uses physical movement right at the beginning of a training session.

└───┘

Procedure

1. Devise six to ten descriptive statements to complete the phrase "Find
   someone who...." Include statements that identify personal information
   and/or training content. Use some of these beginnings:

   Find someone who...

   - likes/enjoys _____
   - knows what a _____ is
   - thinks that _____
   - specializes in _____
   - has already _____
   - is motivated by _____
   - believes that _____
   - has recently read a book about _____
   - has experience with _____
   - dislikes _____
   - has had previous training with _____
   - has a great idea for _____
   - owns a _____
   - wants _____
   - doesn't want _____

2. Distribute the statements to participants and give the following instructions: "This activity is like a scavenger hunt, except that you are looking for people instead of objects. When I say 'begin,' circulate around the room looking for people who match these statements. You can use one person for only one statement, even if he or she matches more than one. When you have found a match, write down the person's first name."

3. When most participants have finished, call a stop to the hunt and reconvene the full group.

4. You may want to offer a token prize to the person who finishes first. More importantly, survey the full group about each of the items. Promote short discussions of some of the items that might stimulate interest in the course topic.

Variations

1. Avoid competition entirely by allowing enough time for everyone to complete the hunt.

2. Ask participants to meet others and find out how many matches can be made with each person.

Case Example

The following scavenger hunt is used for a session on "Active-Training Techniques":

Find someone who...

- has the same first initial as yours
- was born in the same month as you were
- lives in a different state (or country) from yours
- dislikes role playing
- has attended a workshop on training techniques before
- knows what "jigsaw learning" is

When the group is reconvened, go through the alphabet and invite each person whose first initial you just called to stand up and introduce himself or herself. Find out which participant has had the most recent birthday. Hold a brief discussion about the participants' reservations about role playing and what they learned in previous workshops. Invite a participant to explain what "jigsaw learning" is. If no one knows, get participants to speculate what it means and after several guesses, explain it and promise to demonstrate it later on in the workshop.

3 Group Résumé

Overview

Résumés typically describe an individual's accomplishments. A group résumé is a fun way to help participants become acquainted or do some team building with a group whose members already know one another. This activity can be especially effective if the résumé is geared to the subject matter of the training.

Procedure

1. Divide participants into subgroups of three to six members.

2. Tell the group members that they represent an incredible array of talents and experiences!

3. Suggest that one way to identify and brag about the group's resources is to compose a group résumé. (You may want to suggest a job or contract the group could be bidding for.)

4. Give the subgroups newsprint and markers to use in creating their résumés. The résumés should include any information that promotes the subgroup as a whole. The groups may choose to include any of the following information:

    - educational background
    - knowledge about the course content
    - total years of professional experience
    - positions held
    - professional skills
    - major accomplishments
    - publications
    - hobbies, talents, travel, family

5. Invite each subgroup to present its résumé and celebrate the total resources contained within the entire group.

Variations

1. To expedite the activity, give out a prepared résumé outline that specifies the information to be gathered.

2. Instead of having participants compile a résumé, ask them to interview one another about categories that you provide.

Case Example

The following group résumé might be composed by a group in a session on business writing:

WRITERS R US
Todd, Pat, Shawna, Eli
555-6600

Objective
Desire experience with creating and editing professional documents

Qualifications

- Sixteen years in the job market
- Eight years of college education
- Owners of two personal computers
- Familiarity with WordPerfect and Microsoft Word
- Knowledge of: -subject/verb agreement
  -active and passive verbs
  -dangling participles
  -comma usage
  -capitalization
  -commonly misspelled or confused words

- Hobbies include cooking, sunbathing, parasailing, and shopping

4 | Predictions

Overview

This activity is a fascinating way to help participants become acquainted with one another. It is also an interesting experience in first impressions.

Procedure

1. Form subgroups of three or four participants (who are relative strangers to one another).

2. Tell the participants that their job is to predict how each person in their subgroup will answer certain questions you have prepared for them. The following are some all-purpose possibilities:

   - Where did you grow up?

   - What were you like as a child? As a student?

   - Were your parents strict or lenient?

   - What type of music do you enjoy?

   - What are some of your favorite leisure activities?

   - How many hours do you usually sleep nightly?

   Note: Other questions can be added or substituted depending on the group you are leading.

3. Have subgroups begin by selecting one person as the first "subject." Urge participants to be as specific as possible in their predictions about the chosen person. Tell them not to be afraid of bold guesses! As the subgroup members guess, request that the "subject" give no indication as to the accuracy of the predictions. When the predictions about the "subject" are finished, the "subject" should then reveal the answer to each question about himself or herself.

Variations

1. Create questions that require participants to make predictions about one anothers' views and beliefs (rather than factual details).

2. Eliminate the predictions. Instead, invite participants, one by one, to answer the questions immediately. Then, ask subgroup members to reveal what facts about one another "surprised" them (based on their first impressions).

Case Example

An instructor in a math literacy course utilizes prediction questions in an opening class. The class is broken into subgroups of four, with participants predicting answers for the following questions:

- What do you like about math?
- What is difficult about math for you?
- How do you feel about being in this class?

5 Television Commercial

┌─── **Overview** ───┐

This is an excellent opener when group members already
know one another. It can produce rapid team building.
└──────────────────┘

Procedure

1. Divide participants into teams of no more than six members.

2. Ask teams to create a thirty-second television commercial that advertises their team, their profession, or their organization.

3. The commercial should contain a slogan (for example, "Coke's the Real Thing") and visuals.

4. Explain that the general concept and an outline of the commercial is sufficient. But if team members want to act out their commercial, that is fine too.

5. Before each team begins planning its commercial, discuss the characteristics of currently well-known commercials to stimulate creativity (for example, the use of a well-known personality, humor, a comparison to the competition, or sex appeal).

6. Ask each team to present its ideas. Praise everyone's creativity.

Variations

1. Have teams create print advertisements instead of television commercials. Or, if possible, have them actually create commercials on videotape.

2. Invite teams to advertise their interests, values, beliefs, or concerns. Ask the teams to relate these topics to the subject matter of the course.

Case Example

Employees of a hospital are asked to develop a television commercial that advertises the advantages of being a patient at their hospital. They create an advertisement that combines the slogans of several well-known commercials that emphasize care and friendliness, such as "You're in good hands with Southwest Hospital" and "When you care enough to provide the very best."

6 The Company You Keep

──────── **Overview** ────────

This activity introduces physical movement right from
the start and helps participants to get acquainted. It
moves rapidly and is a lot of fun.

Procedure

1. Make a list of categories you think might be appropriate in a getting-
   acquainted activity for the session you are facilitating. Sample categories
   include the following:

   - birthday month

   - negative or positive reaction to [identify a topic, such as poetry, role
     playing, science, or computers]

   - number of hours of nightly sleep

   - favorite [identify any item, such as book, song, or fast food restaurant]

   - left-handed or right-handed writer

   - shoe color

   - agreement or disagreement with any statement of opinion on an issue (for
     example, "Healthcare insurance should be universal.")

2. Clear some floor space so that participants can move around freely.

3. Call out a category. Direct participants to locate as quickly as possible all
   the people whom they would "associate with" given the category. For
   example, "right-handers" and "left-handers" would separate into two
   groups. Or those who agree with a statement would separate from those
   who disagree. If the category contains more than two choices (for example, the month of participants' birthdays), ask participants to congregate
   with those like them, thereby forming several groups.

4. When participants form the appropriate clusters, ask them to shake
   hands with "the company they keep." Invite all the participants to
   observe approximately how many people there are in different groups.

5. Proceed immediately to the next category. Keep the participants moving from group to group as you announce new categories.

6. Reconvene the entire group. Discuss the diversity of participants revealed by the activity.

Variations

1. Ask participants to locate someone who is different from them rather than the same. For example, you might ask participants to find someone who has eyes of a different color from theirs. (Whenever there are not equal numbers of participants in different categories, allow more than one person from one group to cluster with someone from another group.)

2. Invite participants to suggest categories.

Case Example ─────────────────────────────

In a sales training course, a trainer designs a getting-acquainted activity using the following categories:

- likes/dislikes talking on the phone
- thinks "hard sell"/"soft sell" is more effective
- has had no prior sales experience/one to five years of experience/five or more years of experience
- prefers _____ commercial to _____ commercial (provide a choice of two current ones)
- has sold mostly to men/to women/to both equally

7 Really Getting Acquainted

Overview

Most getting-acquainted activities are limited opportunities to meet others. An alternative is to arrange an in-depth experience in which pairs of participants can become really well acquainted.

Procedure

1. Form the participants into pairs in any manner you desire. Criteria for forming pairs might include any of the following:

   - two participants who have never met before
   - two participants who work in different departments or organizations
   - two participants who have different jobs, fields of study, or levels of knowledge or experience

2. Ask the pairs to spend thirty to sixty minutes getting to know each other. Suggest that they go for a walk, have coffee together, or if relevant, visit each other's worksite or office.

3. Supply some questions that the pairs can use to interview each other.

4. When the entire group reconvenes, give pairs a task to do together that enables them to start learning about the subject matter of the session. (See "Ten Assignments to Give Learning Partners," page 18.)

5. Consider the appropriateness of forming the pairs into long-term learning partnerships.

Variations

1. Have participants form trios or quartets instead of pairs.

2. Have participants introduce their partners to the entire group.

Case Example

In the first meeting of a multi-session supervisory training program attended by participants from different divisions and departments, the following ways were established to pair people:

- Level of supervisory experience

    Possible questions: What has changed in this organization over the years?

    What have been the most rewarding experiences you have had? The most difficult?

    How do you feel about recently becoming a supervisor?

- Number of employees to supervise

    Possible questions: When, if ever, do you meet as a group?

    Does a small department have better morale?

    How do you make sure you observe every employee?

- Previous work experience with another company

    Possible questions: How is your former company different from ours?

    What did you like about it? Dislike about it?

    How were supervisors trained at your previous company?

8 Team Getaway

Overview

Often, active training is enhanced by creating long-term learning teams. When this is in your plans, it helps to conduct some initial team-building activities to ensure a solid start. While there are many team-building activities to consider, the following is a favorite.

Procedure

1. Provide each team with a stack of index cards (different sizes in each stack are best).

2. Challenge each team to be as effective a group as possible by constructing a "getaway retreat" solely from the index cards. While folding and tearing the cards are permitted, no other supplies can be used for the construction. Encourage teams to plan their retreat before they begin to construct it. Provide marking pens so that teams can draw on the cards and decorate the getaway as they see fit.

3. Allow at least fifteen minutes for the construction. Do not rush or pressure the teams. It is important for team members to have a successful experience.

4. When the constructions are finished, invite the entire group to take a tour of the getaway retreats. Visit each construction and request that team members show off their work and explain any intricacies of their retreat. Applaud each team's accomplishments. **Do not encourage competitive comparisons among the constructions.**

Variations

1. Ask the teams to build a team "monument" instead of a getaway retreat. Urge them to make the team monument sturdy, high, and aesthetically pleasing.

2. Reconvene the entire group and ask participants to reflect on the experience by responding to this question: "What were some helpful and not so helpful actions we did as a team and individually when working together?"

Case Example

This activity is, of course, an excellent way to begin a training session on the topic of team building. To enhance the learning value, an observer was assigned to each team as it built its getaway. The observer gave feedback about the following:

- goals that evolved (besides getting the job done)
- ways in which members tried to contribute to or block the team effort
- norms that developed about acceptable or unacceptable behavior
- leadership: who had it, who took it, and to whom it was given

9 Reconnecting

┌─── **Overview** ───────────────────────────┐

In a multi-session course, it is sometimes helpful to spend
a few minutes "reconnecting" with participants after
some absence. This activity considers some ways to do this.

└──┘

Procedure

1. Welcome participants back to the course. Explain that you think it might be valuable to spend a few minutes becoming "reconnected" before proceeding with today's session.

2. Pose one or more of the following questions to the participants:

   - What do you remember about our last session? What stands out for you?

   - Have you read/thought out/done something that was stimulated by our last session?

   - What interesting experiences have you had between sessions?

   - What's on your mind right now that might interfere with your ability to give full attention to today's session?

   - How do you feel today? (A fun answer is to use a metaphor, such as "a bruised banana.")

3. Obtain responses by using any one of several formats, such as subgroup discussions or calling on the next speaker. (See "Ten Methods for Obtaining Participation," page 16.)

4. Segue to the topic of the current session.

Variations

1. Conduct a review of the last session instead of posing questions.

2. Present two questions, concepts, or pieces of information covered in the previous session. Ask participants to vote for the one they would most like you to review.

Case Example

A group in a mult-session customer-service course is asked the following questions as it reconvenes:

- What examples of good or poor customer service have you observed since we last met?

- What kinds of customers are the most difficult?

- What feelings do you have now about the value of good customer service?

10 The Great Wind Blows

┌─────────────────── **Overview** ───────────────────┐

This is a fast-paced icebreaker that gets participants moving and laughing. It is a good team builder and allows participants to get to know one another.

└──┘

Procedure

1. Arrange a circle of chairs. Ask each participant to sit in one of the chairs. There should be exactly enough chairs for all participants.

2. Tell the participants that if they agree with your next statement, they should stand up and move to another chair.

3. Stand in the center of the circle and say: "My name is _____ and the great wind blows for everybody who...." Choose an ending that would likely apply to nearly everyone in the class, such as "likes ice cream."

4. At this point, everyone who likes ice cream gets up and runs to an empty chair. As the participants move, make sure you occupy one of the empty seats. If you do, then one participant will have no seat to occupy and will replace you as the person in the center.

5. Have the new person in the center finish the same incomplete sentence, "My name is _____ and the great wind blows for everybody who...," with a new ending. It can be humorous ("sleeps with a night light") or serious ("is worried about the federal deficit").

5. Play the game as often as it seems appropriate to get everyone feeling comfortable with the group.

Variations

1. Provide an extensive list of endings that the participants can use. Include material relevant to the subject matter of the session (everybody

who... "prefers a Macintosh to a PC") or to the job or life experience of the participants (everybody who... "finds nursing stressful").

2. Have pairs of participants in the center instead of just one. Invite them to jointly select an appropriate ending for the sentence.

Case Example

The following endings for the sentence stem were used in a diversity session.

Everybody who...

- has grandparents or parents born outside of the United States
- has ever felt discriminated against
- has ever witnessed discrimination
- is part of a minority group
- has a close friend who is "culturally different"
- would not have been able to work here twenty years ago
- thinks that political correctness has gone too far

11 Setting Ground Rules

Overview

This is a polling method that enables participants to set their own rules for behavior. When participants are part of this team-building process, they are more likely to support the norms that are established.

Procedure

1. Obtain a small number of volunteers (relative to the size of the group) to serve as "interviewers."

2. Have the interviewers circulate throughout the group for a period of ten to fifteen minutes, making contact with as large a sample of people as time permits. Instruct the interviewers to ask group members the following question: "What behaviors do you think would be helpful or not helpful during this session?" (First provide the group with some sample answers to guide responses.)

3. At the end of the allotted time, ask the interviewers to report their findings back to the group. (If desired, list the findings on a flip chart or blackboard.)

4. Usually, it is sufficient to simply hear the collected expressions of the participants to establish a sense of the behavioral ground rules desired by the group. However, it is also possible to analyze the findings, looking for overlap and then consolidating the list.

Variations

1. Provide a list of several possible ground rules. Ask participants to select three from the list. Tabulate the results. The following items might be suitable for your list:

   ■ respect confidentiality

   ■ everyone participates when working in small groups or teams

- observe the starting time of the class
- get to know others different from yourself
- let others finish what they are saying without interrupting
- no "put-downs" or "cheap shots"
- speak for yourself
- be brief and to the point when speaking
- use gender-sensitive language
- be prepared for class
- do not sit in the same seat for every session
- agree to disagree
- give everyone a chance to speak
- build on one anothers' ideas before criticizing them

2. Have the group brainstorm ground rules for participation. Then use a procedure called "multi-voting" to arrive at a final list. Multi-voting is a method for reducing a list of items by one-half. Each participant votes on as many items as he or she wants; the half of the items with the highest number of votes remains on the list. (The procedure can be repeated as often as desired; each vote reduces the list by one-half.)

Case Example

In a several-week-long training program for project teams, the facilitator asks the teams to develop ground rules. The project teams determine that the following rules create an effective working environment:

- Team members must attend all sessions and outside team-project meetings.
- Participants who miss more than two outside meetings will be dropped from the project team.
- The project teams will provide the facilitator with bi-weekly progress reports.
- Teams will provide feedback to one another in review sessions.
- Written summaries of each team's project will be provided to the facilitator and other group members one week prior to the final presentations.

On-the-spot Assessment Strategies

The strategies that follow can be used in conjunction with team-building strategies or by themselves. They are designed to help you learn about the participants while at the same time involving participants right at the beginning of a training session. Some of the strategies allow you to assess specific things about the participants while others are versatile enough to give you an overall picture. On-the-spot assessment strategies are especially useful when you have not had the opportunity to assess the training group prior to the first session. These strategies can also be used to corroborate assessments you have done prior to the training.

12 Assessment Search

Overview

This activity is an interesting way to assess your training group on the spot and, at the same time, involve participants right from the beginning in getting to know one another and working cooperatively.

Procedure

1. Devise three or four questions to help you learn about the participants. You may include questions about the following:

   - their knowledge of the subject matter
   - their attitudes about the subject matter
   - their experiences relevant to the subject matter
   - their skills
   - the nature of their jobs
   - their backgrounds
   - the needs or expectations they bring to this training program

   Frame the questions so that concrete answers are attainable. Avoid open-ended questions.

2. Divide participants into trios or quartets (depending on the number of questions you have created). Give each participant one of the assessment questions. Ask each trio or quartet member to interview the other members and obtain (and record) answers to his or her assigned question.

3. Convene in subgroups all the participants who have been assigned the same question. For example, if there are eighteen participants arranged in trios, six of them will have been assigned the same question.

This strategy was created by Sivasailam Thiagarajan ("Thiagi").

4. Ask each subgroup to pool its data and summarize it. Then, ask subgroup members to report to the entire group what they have learned about one another.

Variations

1. Invite the participants to devise their own questions.

2. Pair up participants, give each pair a list of all the assessment questions, and have pair members interview each other. Poll the full group afterward to obtain results. (This variation is appropriate when dealing with a large group.)

Case Example

Using the above instructions, a trainer conducting a workshop on performance management poses the following three questions:

- What are some common "problem behaviors" you might confront as a supervisor?
- How do you feel when you have to confront a problem employee?
- What actions have you taken in the past to discipline employees?

13 Questions Participants Have

Overview

This is a nonthreatening way to learn about the needs and expectations of participants. It utilizes the response card technique. (See "Ten Occasions to Use Response Cards," page 19.)

Procedure

1. Hand out a blank index card to each participant.

2. Ask the participants to write on the cards any questions they have about the subject matter or the format and goals of the training (names should be withheld).

3. Request that the cards be passed around the group in a clockwise direction. As each card is passed on to the next person, he or she should read it and place a check mark on the card if it contains a question of concern for the reader as well.

4. When a participant's card comes back to him or her, each person will have reviewed all of the group's questions. At this point, identify the questions that received the most votes (checks). Respond to those questions by (a) giving an immediate, but brief answer; (b) postponing the question to a later, more appropriate time in the session; or (c) noting that the session will not be able to address the question (promise a personal response, if possible).

5. Invite some participants to share their questions, even if they did not receive the most votes.

6. Collect the cards for future reference.

Variations

1. If the group is too large to take the time to pass the cards to all participants, break the group into subgroups and follow the same instructions.

Or simply collect the cards without having them passed around and respond to a sample of them.

2. Instead of questions on the index cards, ask participants to write down their hopes and/or concerns about the training, the topics they would like you to cover, or the ground rules for participation they would like to see observed.

Case Example

The following questions are asked in a workshop on HIV/AIDS education:

- About how many people in the world are HIV positive?
- What is the most prevalent way in which HIV is transmitted?
- Are certain ethnic groups more prone to HIV?
- How do children contract HIV since they are not sexually active?
- What is the best medical treatment for AIDS?
- How effective are condoms in preventing HIV transmission?

14 Instant Assessment

Overview

This is an enjoyable, nonthreatening technique to get to know participants. You can use it to "instantly" assess participants' backgrounds, experiences, attitudes, expectations, and concerns.

Procedure

1. Create a set of "responder" cards for each participant. These cards could contain the letters A, B, or C for multiple choice questions, T or F for true/false questions, or numerical ratings such as 1 to 5.

2. Develop a set of statements that participants can respond to with one of their cards. The following are some sample statements:

   - I am taking this course because

     A. I have been sent by my manager.

     B. I am really interested in the topic.

     C. it's a day off from my job.

   - I am concerned that this course will be difficult for me. True or False?

   - I believe that this course will be useful to me in the future.

1	2	3	4	5
strongly disagree				strongly agree

3. Read the first statement and ask participants to respond by holding up the card of their choice.

4. Quickly assess the response. Invite a few participants to share the reasons for their choices.

5. Continue with the remaining statements.

Variations

1. Instead of using cards, ask participants to stand when their choice is announced.

2. Use a conventional show of hands, but add interest by encouraging participants to raise both hands when they strongly agree with a response.

Case Example

In a workshop on delegation skills, the following types of statements can be used:

- I rarely delegate.

1	2	3	4	5
strongly disagree				strongly agree

- Delegation is the process of granting the authority, responsibility, and accountability to an employee to get a job done. True or False?
- I would like to delegate more, but

  A. I am not sure my employees are competent enough.

  B. I am not sure my employees want the added responsibility.

  C. I often convince myself that I can do the task better.

15 A Representative Sample

Overview

Sometimes a training group is very large and it is impossible to quickly get a sense of who is in it. This procedure allows you to draw a representative sampling of the entire group and to get to know these participants by interviewing them publicly.

Procedure

1. Explain that you would like to get to know everyone in the group, but the task would consume too much time.

2. Note that a quicker way to do this would be to create a small sample of participants who represent some of the diversity in the group.

3. Mention some ways in which the participants might be diverse. Ask for a volunteer to be the first member of the "class representative sample." When that person raises his or her hand, ask a few questions to get to know the participant and learn about his or her expectations, skills, job experience, background, opinions, and the like.

4. Having heard the responses of the first volunteer, ask for a second volunteer who is different in some respects from the first volunteer.

5. Continue drawing new volunteers (you decide how many) who are different from those who have previously been interviewed.

Variations

1. Arrange a table and chairs suitably for a panel discussion. Invite each member of the sample to join the panel after he or she has been initially interviewed. When the panel is complete, invite the remaining participants to ask additional questions of the panel.

2. In a multi-session course, invite some participants to meet with you at an off-site location and at a later date so that you can become acquainted. If possible, rotate meetings so that you meet everyone.

Case Example

A representative from the human resource department is about to explain a new benefits plan to a large group of employees. In order to get to know her audience, she begins the session by asking four employees who fit certain criteria to respond to the following questions:

- What is your biggest concern about replacing the old plan?
- What did you like or not like about our previous plan?
- What part of a benefits plan is most important to you?

The first employee is to be a female with more than five years on the job. The second employee is to be a male with a large family. The third employee is to be anyone with less than one year on the job. The fourth employee is to be anyone who thinks he or she is different in viewpoint from any of the previous three.

16 Class Concerns

Overview

Participants usually have some concerns about a course they are attending for the first time, especially if it features active training. This activity allows these concerns to be expressed and discussed openly, yet in a safe manner.

Procedure

1. Tell the participants that you expect they may have concerns about the course. These concerns might include the following:

   - how difficult or time-consuming the work may be
   - how to participate freely and comfortably
   - how participants will function in small learning groups
   - how available the trainer will be
   - what access there will be to reading materials
   - what the time schedule for the course will be

2. List these areas of concern on a board or flip chart. Obtain other concerns from the group.

3. Choose any voting procedure that enables the group to select the top three or four concerns.

4. Form the participants into three or four subgroups. Invite each subgroup to elaborate on one of the concerns. Ask the participants to be specific about the concern.

5. Ask each subgroup to summarize its discussion for the entire group. Obtain reactions.

Variations

1. Ask each subgroup to think of some solutions that either the participants or the trainer can undertake to ease the concern.

2. Rather than end the activity with subgroup reports, create a panel or fishbowl discussion. (See "Ten Methods for Obtaining Participation," page 16.)

Case Example

A trainer for a process-improvement course wants to gauge the concerns of the teams that are attending by requesting their input. After the teams have voted, the following are selected as the top concerns:

- Will management implement the team's decisions?
- What is expected of each team member?
- How will the team resolve issues on which there is considerable disagreement?
- How often will the team meet?

IMMEDIATE LEARNING INVOLVEMENT STRATEGIES ───────

Yet another way to get participants active from the start is to utilize the strategies that follow. They are designed to plunge participants immediately into the subject matter to build interest, arouse curiosity, and stimulate thinking. After all, what good are participants if their brains or, if you will, their "computers" are not ON! Many trainers make the mistake of teaching "too early," before participants are engaged and mentally ready. Using any of these strategies will correct that tendency.

17   Active Knowledge Sharing

Overview

This strategy is a great way to draw participants immediately into the subject matter of the training. You can also use it to assess the knowledge level of participants and to assist in team building. It will work with any group and with any subject matter.

Procedure

1. Provide a list of questions pertaining to the subject matter of the course. You could include some or all of the following categories:

   - terms to define (for example, "What does TQM mean?")

   - people to identify (for example, "Who is Kurt Lewin?")

   - questions concerning actions one could take in certain situations (for example, "How would you deal with an employee who is consistently late?")

   - multiple choice questions concerning facts, concepts, procedures, or policies (for example, "A psychological test is valid if it (a) measures an attribute consistently over time; or (b) measures what it purports to measure.")

   - fill-in-the-blank sentences (for example, "A _____ identifies the basic categories of tasks you can perform with a computer program.")

2. Ask participants to answer the questions as well as they can.

3. Then invite the participants to mill around the room, finding others who have answers that they themselves do not have. Encourage participants to help one another.

4. Reconvene the full group and review the answers. Supply the answers that none of the participants knew.

Variations

1. Hand out an index card to each participant. Ask the participants to write down one piece of information that they are sure is accurate concerning the subject matter of the course. Invite them to mill around, sharing what they wrote on their cards. Encourage them to write down new information garnered from other participants. As a full group, review the information collected.

2. Use opinion questions rather than factual ones. Or mix factual questions with opinion questions.

Case Example

A time-management trainer begins with the following items:

1. Which person is *not* a time-management guru?
   - Alan Lakein
   - Alec Mackenzie
   - W. Edwards Deming

2. What is the biggest time waster reported by managers today?
   - phone interruptions
   - unproductive meetings
   - doing things that could be delegated to others

3. Give an example of a time-management tip contained in self-help books.

4. What is the "Pareto principle?"

5. A study of one thousand business people reported that _____ percent take work home.

6. Why is the "Swiss cheese" method a way to avoid procrastination?

7. One of the most frequently mentioned pieces of time-management advice is to handle incoming memos _____.

18 Rotating Trio Exchange

┌─────────────────────── **Overview** ───────────────────────┐

This is an in-depth way for participants to discuss issues
with some (but usually not all) of their fellow participants. The exchanges can be easily geared to the subject
matter of the training.

└──┘

Procedure

1. Compose a variety of questions that help participants begin discussion of the course content.

2. Divide participants into trios. Position the trios in the room so that each trio can clearly see a trio to its right and to its left. (The best configuration of trios is a circle or square.)

3. Give each trio an opening question (the same question for each trio) to discuss. Select the least threatening question you have devised to begin the trio exchange. Suggest that each person in the trio take a turn answering the question.

4. After a suitable period of discussion, ask the trios to assign a 0, 1, or 2 to each of their members. Direct the participants with the number 1 to rotate one trio clockwise and the participants with the number 2 to rotate two trios clockwise. Ask the participants with the number 0 to remain seated. They will be permanent members of a trio site. Have them raise their hands high so that rotating participants can find them. The result of each rotation will be entirely new trios.

5. Start each new exchange with a new question. Increase the difficulty or sensitivity of the questions as you proceed.

6. You can rotate trios as many times as you have questions to pose and the discussion time to allot. Use the same rotation procedure each time. For example, in a trio exchange of three rotations, each participant will get to meet six other participants in depth.

Variations

1. After each round of questions, quickly poll the participants about their responses before rotating individuals to new trios.

2. Use pairs or quartets instead of trios.

Case Example

In a management training program, a trainer conducts a trio exchange with the following questions:

Round One: How have you been coached by managers in your career? What were effective and ineffective approaches?

Round Two: Give an example of when you have served in a coaching role.

Round Three: What do you want to learn from this workshop?

19 Go to Your Post

┌─────────────────── **Overview** ───────────────────┐

This is a well-known way to incorporate physical movement at the beginning of a course. This technique is flex-
ible enough to use for a variety of activities that are
designed to stimulate initial interest in the training topic.

└──┘

Procedure

1. Post signs around the room. You can use two to create a dichotomous
   choice or several to provide more options.

2. These signs can indicate a variety of preferences:

   - topics of interest to the participants
   - questions about course content
   - solutions to the same problem
   - values
   - personal characteristics or styles
   - authors or well-known people in a field
   - quotations, proverbs, or verses

3. Ask participants to "sign up" for their preference by moving to the place
   in the room where their choice is posted.

4. Have the subgroups that have been created discuss among themselves
   why they have chosen to be in that category. Ask a representative of each
   group to summarize the reasons.

Variations

1. Pair up participants with different preferences and ask them to compare
   their views. Or create a discussion panel with representatives from each
   preference group.

2. Ask each preference group to make a presentation, create an advertisement, or prepare a skit that advocates their preference.

Case Example

This activity can be used at the beginning of a session on coaching.

1. Provide a handout that gives a definition and characteristics of *auditory, visual,* and *kinesthetic* learning styles.

2. Post signs around the room indicating each of the three learning styles.

3. Ask participants to "sign up" under one of the three styles. Urge them to select the style that most accurately describes themselves.

4. Invite the subgroup members to discuss with one another why they see themselves as possessing that style. If one or more of the subgroups is very large, ask those subgroups to subdivide themselves.

5. Next, ask subgroups to discuss what a coach can do to maximize the learning of individuals with their style. (The discussion will be more effective if you pick a specific learning topic as a case in point, such as learning how to use a computer.)

6. Create a panel discussion with a representative from each style category discussing his or her learning needs.

7. Conclude the activity with a discussion about the implications of learning styles for coaching effectiveness.

20 Lightening the Learning Climate

┌─────────────────────── Overview ───────────────────────┐

A training session can quickly achieve an informal,
nonthreatening learning climate by inviting participants
to use creative humor about the subject matter. This
strategy does just that and, at the same time, gets the
participants thinking.

└───┘

Procedure

1. Explain to participants that you want to do an enjoyable opening activity with them before getting serious about the subject matter.

2. Divide the participants into subgroups. Give them an assignment that deliberately asks them to make fun of an important topic, concept, or issue of the training.

3. Examples might be the following:

   - *Organizational Design:* Outline the most oppressive or unworkable organization imaginable.

   - *Business Math:* Develop a list of the most ineffective ways to do mathematical calculations.

   - *Team Building:* Create a skit showing a group or team that is unproductive.

   - *Corporate Grammar:* Write a sentence containing as many grammatical errors as possible.

4. Invite subgroups to present their "creations." Applaud the results.

5. Ask "What did you learn about our subject matter from this activity?"

Variations

1. The trainer can spoof the subject matter with a creation of his or her own making.

2. Create a multiple-choice pretest on the subject of the training. Add humor to the choices given for each item. Ask participants to select the answer for each question that they think could not possibly be right.

Case Example

In a workshop on creative problem solving, participants are asked to brainstorm ways to squelch brainstorming. Among the suggestions that emerge are the following:

- Criticize every idea that does not make sense to you.
- Argue with a person who suggests an idea with which you disagree.
- Ask a question about someone's idea in a tone that implies your disdain.
- Respond with "we've tried that before."
- Complain about the practicality of an idea.
- Make a joke about the idea.

21 Exchanging Viewpoints

Overview

This activity can be utilized to stimulate immediate involvement in the subject matter of your training. It also encourages participants to be careful listeners and to consider diverse viewpoints.

Procedure

1. Give each participant a name tag. Instruct the participants to write their names on the tags and wear them.

2. Ask the participants to introduce themselves to someone else and form pairs. Then, ask the pairs to exchange responses to a provocative question or statement that solicits an opinion about an issue concerning the subject matter of the training.
   An example of a question is "What limits should there be to accommodations made for disabled workers?"
   An example of a statement is "The customer is always right."

3. After an allotted period of time, direct participants to exchange name tags with their partners and then to meet another participant. Instead of introducing themselves, ask participants to share the views of the person who was their previous partner (the person whose name tag they are now wearing).

4. Next, ask participants to switch name tags again and to find another participant to talk to, sharing only the views of the person whose name tag they are wearing.

5. Continue the process until most of the participants have met. Then, tell each participant to retrieve his or her own name tag.

Variations

1. Use this name tag exchange process as a social icebreaker by instructing participants to share background information about themselves rather than viewpoints about a provocative question or statement.

2. Eliminate the exchange of name tags. Instead, ask participants to continue to meet new people, each time hearing their opinions about the question or statement given by you.

Case Example

For a training session on selection interviewing, participants are asked to exchange views on any of the following:

- Do you think it is important to find out if a candidate is married?
- How can you find out whether a candidate is being honest about himself or herself?
- It is hard to avoid the questions you are not allowed to ask by law.
- A good interviewer is a good listener.

22 True or False?

┌─────────────────── **Overview** ───────────────────┐

This collaborative activity stimulates instant involvement
in the subject matter of your session. It also promotes
team building, knowledge sharing, and immediate
learning.

└──┘

Procedure

1. Compose a list of statements relating to your subject matter, half of
   which are true and half of which are false. Write each statement on a
   separate index card. Make sure that there are as many cards as there are
   participants.

2. Distribute one card to each participant. Tell the participants that their
   "mission" is to determine which statements are true and which are false.
   Explain that they are free to use any method to accomplish the task.

3. When the group is finished, have each card read and obtain the group's
   opinion about whether the statement is true or false. Allow for minority
   views!

4. Give feedback about each card and note the ways in which the group
   worked together on the assignment.

5. Indicate that the positive team skills shown will be necessary throughout
   this training course because active learning will be featured.

Variations

1. Before the activity begins, recruit some participants as "observers." Ask
   them to give feedback about the quality of teamwork that emerges.

2. Instead of factual statements, create a list of opinions and place each
   opinion on an index card. Distribute the cards and ask participants to
   attempt to reach a consensus about their reactions to each opinion. Ask
   them to respect minority viewpoints.

Case Example

For a session on "Substance Abuse in the Workplace," the trainer wants to identify what the participants know about the topic. She creates the following statements.

True Statements

- About 50 percent of dysfunctional behavior in the workplace can be attributed to substance abuse.
- Alcohol and drug abuse can be considered disabilities.
- One of the effects of prolonged cocaine use is a sense of fearlessness in the user.
- Regular marijuana use can slow down eye-hand coordination.
- A person who has never used alcohol or drugs can still exhibit behaviors consistent with substance abuse.

False Statements

- Alcohol is not a drug.
- Alcohol is a stimulant.
- It is important that a supervisor be able to diagnose the extent of an employee's alcohol or drug use.
- A corporation has no legal responsibility to assist an employee with substance-abuse problems.
- Drug use in the workplace is a diminishing problem.

23 **Buying into the Course**

```
┌──────────────────── Overview ────────────────────┐
│                                                    │
│  This design provides a way for participants to    │
│  think about and acknowledge their responsibility  │
│  for active learning.                              │
│                                                    │
└────────────────────────────────────────────────────┘
```

Procedure

1. Create copies of the following contract:

I understand that in this course I will be learning about _____
_____ (course subject matter). The objectives
of this course are

- ■ _____

- ■ _____

- ■ _____

- ■ _____

I am committed to these objectives and will strive to do the
following:

- ■ use my time in this course to support these objectives through active participation

- ■ take responsibility for my own learning and not wait for someone else to motivate me

- ■ help others make the most of their learning by listening to what they have to say and offering constructive responses

- ■ think about, review, and apply what I have learned in this course

_____   _____

Signed   Date

---

2. Share with participants your pledge to do everything within your power to make the course an effective learning experience. Provide them with the objectives you intend to help them attain.

3. Distribute copies of the contract to the participants and ask them to read it. Explain that you cannot guarantee the attainment of the objectives without the group's effort and commitment to active learning. Ask the participants to consider the seriousness of this collaboration by agreeing to sign such a written contract with themselves.

4. Provide time for discussion and reflection. Explain that participants will keep their contracts. Leave it up to the participants whether or not to sign the contracts.

Variations

1. Provide a written statement of your responsibilities in this session. Consider some of the following:

   - listen actively to what participants have to say
   - be supportive of participants' attempts to take learning risks
   - vary teaching methods
   - start and end sessions on time
   - supply easy-to-read handouts or other instructional materials
   - be open to participants' suggestions
   - provide visual aids

2. Ask participants to state their expectations of your behavior as the trainer.

Case Example ──────────────────────────

In a course on stress management, the participant contract includes the following commitments:

   - to exercise for twenty minutes three times a week
   - to set aside at least ten minutes of quiet time each day
   - to practice relaxation techniques daily
   - to follow a healthy eating plan

How to Teach Information, Skills, and Attitudes Actively

FULL-CLASS LEARNING

The strategies in this section are designed to enhance full-class instruction. As you will read, even lectures can be made active by utilizing a variety of techniques. You will also find ways to improve the viewing of videos and the appearance of guest presenters. Finally, you will find novel ways to teach difficult concepts and ideas so that the participants' understanding is maximized.

24 **Inquiring Minds Want to Know**

Overview

This simple technique stimulates the curiosity of participants by encouraging speculation about a topic or question. Participants are more likely to retain knowledge about previously uncovered subject matter if they are involved from the onset in a full-class learning experience.

Procedure

1. Ask an intriguing question to the group to stimulate curiosity about a subject you want to discuss. The question posed should be one for which you expect that no participant will know the answer.

   Your question might cover one of the following topics:

   - job-related information (for example, "What are the tell-tale signs of counterfeit currency that a bank teller might notice?")

   - expert theory and research (for example, "According to experts, how many stages do teams go through before they are productive?")

   - terms and definitions (for example, "What does PERT stand for?")

   - specific or technical expertise (for example, "Why would a borrower choose a 7/23 mortgage?")

2. Encourage speculation and guessing. Use terms such as "take a wild guess" or "take a stab."

3. Do not give feedback immediately. Accept all guesses. Build curiosity about the "real answer."

4. Give a lecture in which you present the answer to your question. You should find that participants are more attentive than usual.

Variations

1. Pair up students and ask them to collectively make a guess.

2. Instead of a question, tell students what you are about to teach them and why they should find it interesting. Try to spice up this introduction in somewhat the same fashion as "coming attractions" to a movie.

Case Example

In a management session, the trainer states that the Malcolm Baldrige Award is awarded each year by a committee of experts in recognition of outstanding quality systems. In the past, it has been given to companies such as Xerox, Ames Rubber, and Eastman Chemical. The trainer asks "What do you think are the categories used in the selection process for the Malcolm Baldrige Award?" The group's guesses are recorded and when complete, are compared with the actual list of categories[1]:

- Leadership: *examines senior executives' personal leadership and involvement in creating and sustaining a customer focus and clear and visible quality values*

- Information and Analysis: *examines the scope, validity, management, and use of data and information to drive quality excellence and improve competitive performance*

- Strategic Quality Planning: *examines the company's planning process and how all key quality requirements are integrated into overall business planning*

- Human Resource Development and Management: *examines the key elements of how the company develops and realizes the full potential of the work force to pursue the company's quality and performance objectives*

- Management of Process Quality: *examines the systematic processes the company uses to pursue ever-higher quality and company performance, especially the key elements of process management, including design and management of process quality*

- Quality and Operational Results: *examines the company's quality levels and improvement trends in quality, company operational performance, and supplier quality*

- Customer Focus and Satisfaction: *examines the company's relationships with customers and its knowledge of customer requirements and of the key quality factors that determine marketplace competitiveness*

---

[1] List obtained from the Malcolm Baldrige National Quality Award Office, A537 Administration Building, National Institute of Standards and Technology, Gaithersburg, MD 20899-001.

25 Listening Teams

Overview

This activity is a way to help participants stay focused and alert during a lecture. Listening teams are small groups responsible for clarifying the lecture material.

Procedure

1. Divide the participants into four teams and give the teams these assignments:

Team	Role	Assignment
1	Questioners	After the lecture, ask at least two questions about the lecture material.
2	Agreers	After the lecture, tell which points your team agreed with (or found helpful) and explain why.
3	Nay Sayers	After the lecture, comment on which points your team disagreed with (or found unhelpful) and explain why.
4	Example Givers	After the lecture, explain specific examples or applications of the lecture material.

2. After the lecture, give the teams a few moments to complete their assignments.

3. Call on each team to question, agree, and so forth.

This technique was created by Rebecca Birch and Cynthia Denton-Ade.

Variations

1. Create other roles. For example, ask a team to summarize the lecture or to create questions that test participants' understanding of the lecture.

2. Give out questions in advance that will be answered in the lecture. Challenge participants to listen for the answers. The team that can answer the most questions after the lecture wins.

Case Example

In a lecture on sexual harassment, the instructor includes basic legal information including the following guidelines:

- *Quid Pro Quo Harassment.* Requiring sexual favors in return for job consideration is clearly illegal.

- *Unwelcome Behavior.* It is important to show that the behavior was "unwelcome." There are differences between invited, uninvited-but-welcome, offensive-but-tolerated, and flatly rejected sexual advances.

- *Isolated Occurrences.* Unless the conduct is quite extreme, a single instance or isolated incidents of offensive sexual conduct or remarks generally are not considered to be harassment. As a general rule, the more severe the harassment, the less the need to show that the behavior is repetitive.

- *Hostile Environment.* Touching is not required to meet the definition of sexual harassment. Catcalls, leers, suggestive comments, explicit graffiti, or sexually explicit photographs could be forms of harassment if they contribute to a hostile or offensive work environment.

- *Prior Romantic Involvement.* The fact that two coworkers have, or had at one time, a romantic relationship does not preclude a finding that one has harassed the other.

- *Ordinary Reasonable Woman.* When trying to determine a reasonable standard of offensiveness, women's sensibilities and not men's sensibilities are more appropriate to consider. Courts are beginning to recognize that what is offensive to women may not be disturbing to men. A guideline is beginning to emerge that says that conduct offensive to the "ordinary reasonable woman" should be the standard.

The following are possible team questions or comments:

Questioners	"What does *quid pro quo* literally mean?"
Agreers	"We agree that lewd pictures and off-color jokes are forms of sexual harassment. It is very uncomfortable to have to look at those pictures every day and it is difficult not to be embarrassed by some of the jokes."
Nay Sayers	"We don't think that the standard should be set by women. After all, if they want equality they should be able to 'take it.'"
Example Givers	"We have an example of prior romantic involvement. Two people had been seeing each other. When they broke up, the man continued to pursue the woman to the point of harassment. We think she would have a claim."

26 **Guided Note Taking**

┌─────────────────── **Overview** ───────────────────┐

A popular technique when lecturing is to provide a prepared form that prompts participants to take notes. Even
a minimal gesture such as this engages participants more
than if already completed handouts are provided. There
are a variety of methods to guide note taking. The simplest one involves "filling in the blanks."

└──┘

Procedure

1. Prepare a handout that summarizes the major points of your lecture.

2. Instead of providing a complete text, however, leave portions blank.
   Some of the ways to do this include the following:

   ■ provide a series of terms and their definitions, leaving either the terms
   or their definitions blank

   _____: *a legal standard that states that sexual harassment does not
   have to be physical*

   *Hostile Environment:*_____

   ■ leave one or more of a series of points blank

   The Roles of a Team Facilitator

   • _____

   • _____

   • _____

   • _____

   ■ omit key words from a short paragraph

   *Today, managers often face problems such as low _____, high
   _____, and _____ quality of service. Traditional
   management solutions often tend, like the _____ _____, to
   generate _____ new problems for every one that is solved.*

3. Distribute the handout to the participants. Explain that you have created the blanks to help the group listen actively to your presentation and suggest that the participants use their active-listening skills to complete the handout.

Variations

1. Provide a work sheet that lists the major subtopics of your presentation. Leave plenty of space for note taking. The result will look something like the following:

Four Types of Leadership Styles

Directing:

Coaching:

Supporting:

Delegating:

(Optional) After the presentation, distribute a second copy of the handout with blanks. Challenge the participants to fill in the blanks without looking at their notes.

2. Divide a lecture into several sections. Ask participants to listen intently while you are speaking but not to take notes. Invite them instead to write down notes during the breaks in the lecture.

Case Example

For a training session on delegation, the trainer distributes a handout entitled "The Do's and Don'ts of Delegation." The handout format is a T-chart: one column is labeled "Do Delegate" and the other "Do Not Delegate."

As the lecture is given, participants make notes on the chart. When completed by the participants, the chart looks like this:

DO DELEGATE	DO NOT DELEGATE
■ all routine or sporadic clerical duties ■ minor decisions ■ routine questions ■ minor staffing problems ■ anything your subordinates are expected to do when you are not there	■ an emergency or short-term task for which there is no time to explain or train ■ morale problems ■ assignments from your boss that he or she expects you to do personally ■ a job no one else in the unit is qualified to do ■ hiring, firing, or disciplinary matters

27 Lecture Bingo

Overview

A lecture can be less boring and participants will be more alert if you make the lecture into a game. Key points are discussed while participants play bingo.

Procedure

1. Create a lecture with up to nine key points.

2. Develop a bingo card that contains these key points on a 3 x 3 grid. Place a different point in each of the boxes. If you have fewer than nine key points, leave some boxes empty.

3. Create additional bingo cards with the same key points but place the points in different boxes. The result should be that few, if any, bingo cards are alike.

4. Distribute the bingo cards to the participants. Also provide participants with a strip of nine self-sticking colored dots (approximately, $\frac{1}{2}$" to $\frac{3}{4}$" in diameter). Instruct the participants that as your lecture proceeds from point to point, they should place a dot on their cards for each point that you discuss. (*Note:* Empty boxes cannot be covered with a dot.)

5. As participants collect three vertical, horizontal, or diagonal dots in a row, they yell "bingo!"

6. Complete the lecture. Allow participants to obtain bingo as many times as they can.

Variations

1. Use key terms or names mentioned in your lecture (rather than key points) as the basis for the bingo cards. When the term or name is first mentioned, participants can place a sticker in the appropriate box.

2. Create a 2 x 2 bingo grid. Continue to discuss several key points, terms, or names in your lecture. Indicate only four of these on any one bingo

card. Try to make few, if any, cards alike by including different information on each card.

Case Example

In a lecture on time-management tips, the trainer includes the following main points:

- Carry 3 x 5 cards or a small spiral notebook to jot down notes and ideas.
- Skim books and articles quickly, looking for ideas. Tear out or photocopy articles of interest and file them appropriately for future reference.
- Carry a hand-held tape recorder with you to record ideas and reminders. This is particularly useful when you are driving a car.
- Create a "To Read" file and carry it with you when you travel or know you may be kept waiting for an appointment.
- Make an appointment with yourself to complete a task and block off the time on your calendar.
- Save up trivial matters for a three-hour session once a month.
- Group phone calls. Set aside a particular time of the day to make all your calls.
- List what you want to say before placing a phone call. You will not then forget important points and will avoid being lured into idle chit-chat.
- Try to find a new technique every day that will help you gain time.

SAMPLE BINGO CARD:

Carry "To Read" file	Schedule three-hour session for trivial tasks	Tear out/ photocopy articles
Carry 3 x 5 cards	Make appointment with self	List points to discuss on telephone
Group phone calls	Carry hand-held recorder	Find a new time-saving technique every day

28 Synergetic Teaching

Overview

This method is a real change of pace. It allows participants who have had different experiences learning the same material to compare notes.

Procedure

1. Divide the participants into two equal subgroups.

2. Send one subgroup to another room to read about the topic you are teaching. Make sure the reading material is well-formatted and easy to read.

3. During this time, give a lecture on the same material to the other subgroup.

4. Next, reverse learning experiences. Provide reading material on your topic for the subgroup that has heard the lecture and provide a lecture for the reading subgroup.

5. Pair up a member from each subgroup and have the pairs recap what they have learned.

Variations

1. Ask half of the participants to listen to a lecture with their eyes closed while the other half views visual information such as overhead transparencies accompanying the lecture with their ears covered. After the lecture is completed, ask the participants to compare notes about what they have heard or seen.

2. Give one half of the participants concrete examples of a concept or theory you want them to learn. Do not explain the concept or theory itself. Present to the other half of the participants the concept or theory without the examples. Pair up participants from both groups and have them review the lesson together.

Case Example

In a course on business insurance, accountants are learning about "loss exposures" and their impact on business assets and income/capital. One half of the participants are given the following chart and asked to study it with a learning partner so that they can each share the examples it contains with a participant in the other half of the group.

Types of Loss Exposure
1. sudden, often violent occurrences that a business can be exposed to occasionally— such as fire, flood, wind, vandalism, weight of snow/ice, or frozen pipes
2. exposures of the premises or operations, product liability, directors' and officers' losses, professional liability loss
3. employee dishonesty, injury of employees, computer losses
4. fines, closures, prosecution, added costs in construction, taxes

Meanwhile, the instructor is giving the other half of the group a brief lecture on the four categories of loss exposures (without examples):

Categories of Loss Exposure
1. External
2. Legal
3. Internal
4. Government

Participants from each half of the group are paired up. They tell each other what they have learned and, together, attempt to sort the examples into the four categories. All participants then reconvene and review what they have learned synergetically.

29 Guided Teaching

```
┌─────────────────── Overview ───────────────────┐
│                                                 │
│  In this technique, the trainer asks one or     │
│  more questions to tap the knowledge of the     │
│  participants or to obtain their hypotheses     │
│  or conclusions and then sorts the re-          │
│  sponses into categories. The guided-teaching   │
│  method is a nice break from straight           │
│  lecturing and allows the trainer to learn      │
│  what participants already know and understand   │
│  before making instructional points. This       │
│  method is espe-cially useful when teaching      │
│  abstract concepts.                             │
│                                                 │
└─────────────────────────────────────────────────┘
```

Procedure

1. Pose a question or a series of questions that taps into the thinking and existing knowledge of participants. Utilize questions that have several possible answers, such as "How can you tell how intelligent someone is?"

2. Give the participants some time in pairs or subgroups to consider their responses.

3. Reconvene the entire group and record the participants' ideas. If possible, sort their responses into separate lists that correspond to different categories or concepts you are trying to teach. In the example question above, you might list an idea such as "the ability to rebuild an engine" under the category *motoric intelligence.*

4. Present the major concepts of the course. Have participants figure out how their responses relate to these points. Note any of the participants' ideas that add to the course content.

Variations

1. Do not sort participants' responses into separate lists. Instead, create one continuous list and ask the participants to categorize their own ideas before you compare the ideas to the concepts you will present.

2. Begin the lesson without predetermined categories. Ask the participants to work with you to sort ideas into useful categories.

Case Example

In a session on effective meetings, the trainer posts a piece of flip-chart paper entitled "Bad Meetings."

The participants are asked to recall their own experiences in bad meetings and to discuss these experiences in pairs.

The participants then share their experiences with the entire group while the trainer records their responses on the flip-chart paper. Responses are as follows:

Bad Meetings

- no one was prepared
- started late
- had no scheduled ending
- digressed from the subject
- did not have an agenda
- one person dominated
- few participated
- no one talked
- no assignments were given

The trainer then points out that bad meetings are the result of failures at three points in time:

- before the meeting
- during the meeting
- after the meeting

The points made by the participants are then placed under the most appropriate category. For example, "no one was prepared" is a "before meeting" breakdown. The trainer then discusses how the effectiveness of meetings is a result of careful attention to all three time periods.

30 Meet the Pros

Overview

This activity is an excellent way to involve subject-matter experts or guest speakers who do not have the time or expertise to prepare for a session. At the same time, it gives participants the opportunity to interact with a subject-matter expert in a unique way and to take an active role in preparing for the guest speaker.

Procedure

1. Invite a guest speaker who is an expert on the subject of the session to address the group. (For example, an employment interviewer might visit a career-development class, or a loan officer could be the guest speaker for a group of bank customer-service representatives.)

2. Prepare the guest speaker by telling him or her that the session will be conducted like a press conference. In keeping with that format, the speaker is to prepare a few brief remarks or an opening statement and then be prepared to answer questions from "the press."

3. Prior to the guest's appearance, prepare the participants by discussing how a press conference is conducted, and then giving them an opportunity to formulate several questions to ask the speaker.

Variations

1. Choose to have several guests at the same session and conduct round-table discussions. Seat each speaker at a table or in a circle of chairs to share information and experiences with a small group. The group members will have an opportunity to interact with the expert by asking questions in a more personal environment. Divide the session into a series of "rounds." Determine the length of each round depending on the time available for the session and the number of guests. In general, ten or fifteen minutes for each round is appropriate. Direct each small group to move from one guest to the next as the rounds progress.

2. Invite some participants from a previous training group to serve as visiting speakers.

Case Example

In a new-employee orientation session at a large bank, representatives from various departments are seated at tables and share with small groups of new employees on a rotating basis what their departments do and how they fit into the overall operation. The following areas are represented: operations, branch administration, marketing, investments, management information systems, auditing, accounting, human resources, consumer lending, and commercial lending.

Each department representative distributes handouts that include the following information:

- names and phone numbers of key people in the department and what they do

- an organization chart

- a brief description of the department's function

During each round, the department representative gives a brief overview of his or her department and then solicits questions "press conference style" from the new employees.

31 Acting Out

Overview

Sometimes, no matter how clear a lecture is or how descriptive visual aids are, certain concepts and procedures are not understood. One way to help clarify the material is to ask some participants to act out the concepts or walk through the procedures you are trying to explain.

Procedure

1. Choose a concept (or a set of related concepts) or a procedure that can be illustrated by acting it out. Some examples include the following:

   - an office requisition procedure
   - a project-management planning tool
   - a feedback loop
   - a hidden agenda in a team meeting

2. Use any of the following methods to act out the concept:

   - Have some participants come to the front of the room and ask each of them to physically simulate an aspect of the concept or procedure.
   - Create large cards that name the parts of a procedure or concept. Distribute the cards to some participants. Ask the participants with cards to arrange themselves so that the steps of the procedure are correctly sequenced.
   - Develop a role play in which participants dramatize the concept or procedure.
   - Ask participants to volunteer to demonstrate a procedure that involves several people.

3. Discuss the learning drama that participants have created.

Variations

1. Videotape a group of people illustrating the concept or procedure and show it to the participants.

2. Ask participants to create a way to act out a concept or procedure without your guidance.

Case Example

A team-building trainer utilizes the following activity, "The Team Machine," to help participants understand several points about teamwork.

The Team Machine[1]

Say the following to participants:

- Lift your right hand and move it as if you are clapping. Listen to the sound of one hand clapping.

- Raise your left hand and clap with both hands. If your task is to clap, wouldn't you want to use all of your available resources?

- This is an example of how the human system operates on an individual level. Each person has several parts and the parts work together to accomplish a task.

- There are other types of systems. Imagine a six-cylinder car—a well-timed, synchronized machine. Each cylinder fires in sequence so that the system can function.

- Imagine this automobile running on only five cylinders. What would happen to the power? Or what if you put the plug wires on haphazardly?

- Organizational teams are just like individuals and automobiles. The teams work best when they use all of their resources, when there is a plan, and when they have a coordinated system for accomplishing tasks.

- Let's experiment. Watch me as I stand here making a motion and a sound with my voice. Let's pretend we're making a human machine, a well-timed machine.

  (Choose the first participant.)

- Please come up here.

  (Point to a large, empty place in the room.)

---

[1] This exercise was developed by Jeffrey D. Kindler.

- Now I would like you to make a unique sound with your voice, place one hand out in front of you, and make a motion with your body. Good.

  (Ask the remaining participants to come up one at a time and arrange themselves in a circle.)

  (To each member say the following:)

- Make a different sound, a different motion, and use one hand to connect yourself to the person in front of you.

  (After the circle is complete, say the following:)

- Continue making your interesting sounds and motions. Notice how you take turns, how you bob and weave or wax and wane.

- Here are some things to think about.

  - Have we somehow woven ourselves into a pattern in which we all contribute our vocal and motor skills?

  - Is the sum more than the parts?

  - Are we synchronized?

  - Is there a group system here, something bigger, more complex than each individual?

- Now we have a system for working together. This is the hallmark of an effective team.

32 | What's My Line?

Overview

This activity offers a fresh approach to helping participants learn cognitive material. By adapting an old television game show, participants have an opportunity to review material that has just been taught and to test one another as a reinforcement to your lesson.

Procedure

1. Divide the group into two or more teams.

2. Write on separate slips of paper any of the following statements:

   - I am [supply a person]. For example, *I am Malcolm Knowles.*
   - I am [supply an event]. For example, *I am a performance review.*
   - I am [supply a theory]. For example, *I am social learning theory.*
   - I am [supply a concept]. For example, *I am synergy.*
   - I am [supply a skill]. For example, *I am brainstorming.*

3. Put these slips of paper in a box and ask each team to choose one slip. The chosen slip reveals the identity of the "mystery guest."

4. Give the teams five minutes to do the following tasks:

   - Choose a team member to be the mystery guest.
   - Anticipate questions he or she will be asked and think of responses.

5. Select the team that will present the first mystery guest.

6. Create a panel of participants from other teams (by whatever method you choose).

7. Begin the game. Ask the mystery guest to reveal his or her category (person, event, theory, concept, or skill). The panelists take turns asking "yes" or "no" questions of the mystery guest until one of the panelists is able to identify the guest.

8. Invite the remaining teams to present their mystery guests. Create a new panel for each guest.

Variations

1. Allow each mystery guest to consult with his or her teammates if he or she is unsure how to answer the questions posed by the panelists.

2. Specify how you want the mystery guest to act. For example, a guest might try to impersonate the famous person being portrayed.

Case Example

Near the end of a program on total quality management, the trainer writes the names of the following group-process tools on separate slips of paper:

- Round Robin Brainstorming
- Nominal Group Technique
- Mindmapping
- Decision-Making Matrix
- Multi-Voting
- Force-Field Analysis

Each team receives one of the slips of paper and team members discuss among themselves what questions they might be asked and how they might respond. The teams may focus on benefits, characteristics, and uses of the tools. To make the activity interesting and to make sure participants are focusing on the various characteristics of the group-process tools, the trainer instructs the panelists to ask at least three questions before guessing the identity of the mystery guest. The questions the "mindmapping" team anticipates and the team's responses are as follows:

Question	Answer
Are you structured?	No
Are you spontaneous?	Yes
Do you use colors?	Yes
Are you mindmapping?	Yes

33 | Video Critic

Procedure

1. Select a video that you want to show participants.

2. Tell participants, prior to watching the video, that you want them to review the video critically. Ask them to look at several factors, including the following:

   - realism of situation
   - practicality
   - unforgettable moments
   - organization of content
   - applicability to work situation

3. Show the video.

4. Conduct a discussion you might call "critic's corner."

5. (Optional) Poll the class using some kind of overall rating system, such as one to five stars or thumbs up, thumbs down.

Variations

1. Create a panel of video reviewers.

2. Show the video again. Sometimes, critics change their minds on second viewing.

Case Example

A trainer shows the video "You'll Soon Get the Hang of It" (Video Arts) for a humorous look at on-the-job training. The trainer explains that it is a British film with the dry wit of John Cleese. Participants are given a sheet of paper with the following questions:

- How realistic was the situation?
- Did the British accents affect the video's impact?
- Did the humor add to or detract from the subject matter?
- What scene in the video had the most impact?
- How do the events in the video relate to anything you have experienced on the job?

The trainer asks the participants to jot down answers to the questions as they watch the video. After the video, the trainer conducts a discussion using the questions as a guide.

During the discussion, participants note that a particularly significant scene is the one in which the new employee is not given any background information on his assigned task of stacking boxes on a shelf. He has not been given the "big picture." In order to save space, he places the boxes on their sides, only to be reprimanded by his supervisor. It seems the boxes must be placed upright to prevent their contents from exploding.

After discussing the remaining questions, the group is asked to give the video a thumbs up or a thumbs down to indicate how well the video illustrates the importance of a structured approach to on-the-job training.

STIMULATING DISCUSSION

All too often, a trainer tries to stimulate discussion but is met with uncomfortable silence as participants wonder who will dare to speak up first. Starting a discussion is no different from beginning a lecture. You first have to build interest! The strategies that follow are certain to stimulate discussion. Some will even create heated, but manageable, exchanges between participants. All of them are designed so that *every* participant is involved.

34 Active Debate

Overview

A debate can be a valuable method for promoting thinking and reflection, especially if participants are expected to take a position that may be contrary to their own. This design actively involves every participant, not just the debaters.

Procedure

1. Develop a statement that takes a position with regard to a controversial issue relating to your subject matter. For example, "There is too much new drug development today."

2. Divide the group into two debating teams. Assign (arbitrarily) the "pro" position to one team and the "con" position to the other.

3. Next, create two to four subgroups within each debating team. In a class of twenty-four participants, for example, you might create three pro subgroups and three con subgroups, each containing four members. Ask each subgroup to develop arguments for its assigned position. At the end of its discussion, have each subgroup select a spokesperson.

4. Set up two facing rows of two to four chairs each (depending on the number of subgroups created for each position) for the spokespersons of each team. Place the remaining participants behind their spokespersons. For the example above, the arrangement will look like this:

```
x                          x
x                          x
x                          x
x  pro              con    x
x  pro              con    x
x  pro              con    x
x                          x
x                          x
x                          x
```

Begin the debate by having the spokespersons present their views. Refer to this process as "opening arguments."

5. After everyone has heard the opening arguments, stop the debate and reconvene the original subgroups. Ask the subgroups to strategize how to counter the opening arguments of the opposing side. Again, have each subgroup select a spokesperson, preferably a new person.

6. Resume the debate. Have the spokespersons give "counterarguments." As the debate continues (be sure to alternate between sides), encourage other participants to pass notes to their debaters with suggested arguments or rebuttals. Also, urge them to cheer or applaud the arguments of their debate-team representatives.

7. When you think it appropriate, end the debate. Instead of declaring a winner, reconvene the entire group in a circle. Be sure to integrate the group by having participants sit next to people who were on opposing teams. Hold a full-group discussion on what participants learned about the issue from the debate experience. Also, ask participants to identify what they thought were the best arguments raised on both sides.

Variations

1. Add one or more empty chairs to the spokespersons' rows. Allow participants to occupy these empty chairs whenever they want to join the debate.

2. Start the activity immediately with the opening arguments of the debate. Proceed with a conventional debate, but frequently rotate the debaters.

Case Example ━━━━━━━━━━━━━━━━━━━━━━━━━━━━━━━

In a course on business ethics, the trainer writes on a flip chart, "Making personal calls on company time using a company telephone is unethical."

The group is then divided into two teams with one team taking the pro position and the other, the con. Each team is divided into subgroups to discuss opening arguments. The spokesperson for each subgroup has an opportunity to make brief opening remarks.

Opening remarks for the pro side include the following:

■ Everyone does it.

- Because people are at work all day, they have to have some way to conduct personal business.
- It doesn't cost the company much money in comparison to the big picture.

Arguments for the con side are as follows:

- Businesses lose money paying for employees' personal calls.
- Productivity is reduced when employees spend time on personal calls.
- If the practice weren't unethical, companies wouldn't establish policies regarding personal calls.

After the opening remarks, the subgroups reconvene to discuss counterarguments. The debate then resumes with new debaters.

35 Town Meeting

Overview

This discussion format is well suited for large groups. By creating an atmosphere akin to a "town meeting," the entire group can become involved in the discussion.

Procedure

1. Select an interesting topic or case problem concerning your subject matter. Briefly present the topic or problem as objectively as possible, giving background information and an overview of different viewpoints. If you wish, provide documents that illuminate the topic or problem.

2. Point out that you would like to obtain the participants' views on the matter. Instead of your calling on each participant, explain that you will be following a format entitled "call on the next speaker." Whenever someone is finished speaking, that person should look around the room and call on someone else who also wishes to speak (as indicated by a raised hand).

3. Urge participants to keep their remarks brief so that as many others as possible can participate in the town meeting. Establish a time limit, if you wish, for the length of a speaker's turn. Direct participants to call on someone who has not previously participated before choosing someone who has already spoken.

4. Continue the discussion as long as it seems of value.

Variations

1. Organize the meeting into a debate. Invite participants to sit on one side of the room or the other, depending on their positions on the controversy. Follow the call-on-the-next-speaker format with the instruction that the next speaker must have an opposing point of view. Encourage participants to move to the other side of the room if their views are swayed by the debate.

2. Begin the town meeting with a panel discussion. Have the panelists present their own views and then call on speakers from the audience.

Case Example ───

In a training session for first-level supervisors, the trainer presents a brief lecture about three different approaches to employee motivation. The trainer uses props to illustrate and represent each approach.

The first approach is represented by a whip; the second by a carrot dangling on a string from a big stick; the third by a live flowering plant.

The trainer asks for volunteers to explain what is meant by each of the three methods represented. Participants suggest the following explanations:

- The whip represents threat and fear of punishment.

- The carrot on a stick represents promises and incentives.

- The flowering plant suggests an environment in which employees are encouraged to grow and develop.

The trainer asks for someone to begin the discussion by commenting on the message and the metaphor of each method and giving examples of and opinions concerning the effectiveness of each method.

Others who wish to comment raise their hands, and the speaker calls on someone else. That speaker in turn calls on the next speaker. This continues until all three viewpoints have been adequately addressed.

36 Three-Stage Fishbowl Discussion

> **Overview**
>
> A fishbowl is a discussion format in which a portion of
> the group forms a discussion circle and the remaining
> participants form a listening circle around the discussion
> group. (See "Ten Methods for Obtaining Participation,"
> page 16.) Below is one of the more interesting ways to
> set up a fishbowl discussion.

Procedure

1. Devise three questions for discussion relevant to your subject matter.
   Ideally, the questions should be interrelated but that is not required.
   Decide in what order you would like the questions discussed.

2. Arrange chairs in a fishbowl configuration (two concentric circles). Have
   the participants count off by 1's, 2's, and 3's (or use another method for
   creating three groups, as suggested in "Ten Strategies for Forming Groups,"
   page 23). Ask the members of Group 1 to occupy the discussion-circle
   seats and ask the members of groups 2 and 3 to sit in the outer-circle
   seats. Pose your first question for discussion. Allow up to ten minutes for
   discussion. If you wish, invite a participant to facilitate the discussion.

3. Next, invite the members of Group 2 to sit in the inner circle, replacing
   Group 1 members who now move to the outer circle. Ask the members
   of Group 2 if they would like to make any brief comments about the first
   discussion and then segue into the second discussion topic.

4. Follow the same procedure with members of the third discussion group.

5. When all three questions have been discussed, reconvene the entire group.
   Ask the participants for their reflections about the entire discussion.

Variations

1. If it is not possible to have circles of chairs, have a rotating panel discussion instead. One third of the group become panelists for each discus-

       101 Ways to Make Training Active

sion question. The panelists can sit in front of the room facing the remainder of the participants. If you are using a U-shaped classroom arrangement or a conference table (see "Ten Layouts for Setting Up a Training Classroom," page 5), designate a side of the table for the panel group.

2. Use only one discussion question rather than three. Invite each subsequent group to respond to the discussion of the preceding group.

Case Example

A session on customer service addresses the following three questions:

1. What have been your best experiences as a customer?

2. What do our customers want and expect?

3. What are some specific strategies and behaviors the customer-service representative should use to meet and exceed the customers' needs and expectations?

The participants count off by 1's, 2's, and 3's, and the members of Group 1 occupy the chairs in the inner circle with the other participants sitting in the outer circle.

Members of Group 1 share their own personal experiences as customers. The examples they give that contributed to their positive experiences include the following:

- friendly service
- extraordinary effort
- satisfactory recovery from errors
- immediate attention

After Group 1 completes its discussion, members of Group 2 replace members of Group 1 in the inner circle. They discuss customer expectations and conclude that the company's customers want the following:

- responsiveness
- reliability
- accuracy
- friendliness
- a pleasant environment

- empathy
- competency
- fairness

Group 3 replaces Group 2 and suggests the following behaviors for meeting or exceeding customers' expectations:

- using each customer's name
- returning calls promptly
- sending error-free correspondence
- smiling
- asking how to be of help

The entire group reconvenes to discuss how well the participants feel they are doing in meeting the customers' expectations through the desired behaviors.

37 **Expanding Panel**

> **Overview**
>
> This activity is an excellent way to stimulate discussion and active participation while giving participants an opportunity to identify, explain, and clarify issues.

Procedure

1. Select an issue that will engage the participants' interest. Present the issue so that participants will be stimulated to discuss their viewpoints. Identify up to five questions for discussion.

2. Choose four to six people to serve as a panel-discussion group. Ask them to sit in a semicircle at the front of the room.

3. Ask the remaining participants to position themselves on three sides of the discussion group in a horseshoe arrangement.

4. Begin with a provocative opening question. Moderate a panel discussion with the core group while the observers take notes in preparation for their own discussions.

5. At the end of the designated discussion period, separate the entire group into subgroups to continue the discussion of the remaining questions.

Variations

1. Reverse the sequence; begin with small-group discussion and follow with a panel discussion.

2. Invite the participants to generate the questions for discussion.

Case Example

In a session on managing change, the trainer introduces the subject by explaining that people naturally resist change, but that change is inevitable. To deal with change, we have to understand it. The trainer asks for five volunteers to serve as panelists and directs them to sit in a semicircle with the rest of the participants seated around them in a horseshoe configuration. The trainer then poses the following question to the panelists:

- What types of changes are you and/or your employees experiencing?

After fifteen minutes of listening to the panelists discuss the question, the trainer divides the participants into subgroups and asks them to discuss the following questions:

- What are the effects of change on you and other employees?
- Why do people resist change?
- What are the positive aspects of change?
- What are the negative aspects of change?

The entire group is then reconvened to obtain highlights of the subgroup discussions.

38 Point-Counterpoint

Overview

This activity is an excellent technique to stimulate discussion and gain a deeper understanding of complex issues. The format is similar to a debate but is less formal and moves more quickly.

Procedure

1. Select an issue that has two or more sides.

2. Divide the participants into subgroups according to the number of positions you have stated and ask each subgroup to come up with arguments to support its position. Encourage subgroup members to work with a partner or in small cluster groups.

3. Reconvene the entire group, but ask members of each subgroup to sit together with space between the subgroups.

4. Explain that any participant can begin the debate. After that participant has had an opportunity to present **one** argument in favor of his or her assigned position, allow a different argument or counterargument from a member of another subgroup. Continue the discussion, making sure that all positions are presented.

5. Conclude the activity by offering comparisons of the different positions. Allow for follow-up reaction and discussion.

Variations

1. Instead of a full-group debate, pair up individual participants from different subgroups and have them argue with each other. This can be done simultaneously, so that every participant is engaged in the debate at the same time.

2. Line up two opposing subgroups so that they are facing each other. As one person concludes his or her argument, have that participant then toss an

object (such as a ball or a beanbag) to a member of the opposing side. The person catching the object must rebut the previous person's argument.

Case Example

In a session on business reengineering, the trainer divides the participants into two subgroups. Group A is given the "pro" position and Group B is given the "con" position. Each subgroup is asked to think of points to support its assigned position for the following statement:

"We are overdoing the use of teams in our organization."

The exchange is as follows:

Group A *Point:* "We're wasting too much time in team meetings."

Group B *Counterpoint:* "It's going to take a while to learn how to run meetings more effectively."

Group A *Point:* "This is an excellent opportunity to empower employees."

Group B *Counterpoint:* "We're doing tasks and making decisions that managers are paid to do."

39 Reading Aloud

──────── **Overview** ────────

Surprisingly, reading a text aloud can help participants to focus mentally, raise questions, and stimulate discussion. This strategy is much like a Bible-study session. It has the effect of focusing attention and creating a cohesive group.

Procedure

1. Choose a text that is sufficiently interesting to read aloud. Limit yourself to a selection that is less than five hundred words.

2. Introduce the text to the participants, highlighting key points or issues to be raised.

3. Section off the text by paragraphs or some other means. Invite volunteers to read aloud different sections.

4. As the reading progresses, stop when appropriate to emphasize certain points, raise or entertain questions, or give examples. Allow brief discussions if participants show an interest in certain portions. Then, proceed with the reading.

Variations

1. Do the reading yourself if you feel it will enhance the presentation of the text or if you have concerns about the reading skills of participants.

2. Form participants into pairs. Have the members of each pair read to each other, stopping for clarification and discussion as they see fit.

Case Example ─────────────────────────────

In a business etiquette class, the instructor distributes copies of George Washington's "Rules of Civility and Decent Behavior In Company and Conversations" written in the 1700s. From the list of 110 rules, the instructor chooses those rules that are relevant to today's business world. As each participant takes a turn reading a passage, he or she comments on how and why these points of etiquette are appropriate today.

Following are some samples of the text and the participants' analysis:

- "When you meet with one of Greater Quality than yourself, Stop, and retire especially if it be at a Door or any Straight place to give way for him to Pass."

The participant reading this rule relates it to the practice of allowing a person of higher rank to proceed through a door first. A discussion ensues as to whether such deference is still necessary given today's egalitarian values.

- "If others talk at Table, be attentive but talk not with Meat in your Mouth."

The participant describes this as a basic principle taught in childhood and applicable in any situation. Others agree.

40 Trial by Jury

Overview

This technique utilizes a mock trial complete with witnesses, prosecutors, defenders, friends of the court, and more. It is a good method to spark "controversy learning," that is, the process of learning by effectively arguing a viewpoint and challenging the opposite view.

Procedure

1. Create an indictment that will help participants see the different sides of an issue. Examples of "crimes" for which someone might be tried are an unproven theory, a value that does not have merit, a faulty process, or a moral failing.

2. Assign roles to participants. Depending on the number of participants, you could use all or some of these roles: defendant, defense attorney, defense witness, prosecuting attorney, prosecution witness, friend of the court, judge, and jury member. Each role can be filled by one person or by a team. You could have any number on the jury.

3. Allow time for participants to prepare. This could be a from a few minutes to an hour, depending on the complexity of the issue.

4. Conduct the trial. Consider using the following activities: opening arguments, presentations by the prosecutor and witnesses, friend-of-the-court briefs, and closing arguments.

5. Conduct the jury deliberations. These should be done publicly, so everyone can hear how the evidence is being weighed. Participants who are not members of the jury can be given an assignment to listen for various aspects of the case.

This technique was created by Rebecca Birch and Cynthia Denton-Ade.

Variations

1. Extend the activity by staging a retrial.

2. Eliminate a trial by jury and substitute a trial by judge only.

Case Example ─────────────────────────────

In a session on performance management, a trainer states that the manager has been indicted on charges of "surprising" the employee with his review. In other words, the employee had not been told of his poor performance until the formal performance review.

- The trainer assigns the roles of defendant, defense attorney, defense witnesses, prosecuting attorney, prosecution witnesses, and judge.

- The four prosecution witnesses meet as a group to determine strategies and to prepare their testimony. The prosecution witnesses are employees (past and present) of the defendant as well as enlightened managers who practice true performance management and coach their employees throughout the review period.

- The three defense witnesses also meet to discuss strategy. These witnesses are other managers who conduct their reviews in the same way as the defendant.

- The rest of the group serves as the jury.

- The prosecution and its witnesses stress the importance of coaching techniques and other good management principles and practices including mutual goal setting, feedback, and performance monitoring.

- The defense builds its case based on the acceptance of traditional management practices and the "grade card" approach to evaluating performance.

Prompting Questions ───────

"Are there any questions?" asks the trainer. All too often what follows is silence. Some trainers may think the participants aren't interested. Others may conclude that everything must be clear. Unfortunately, the truth is often that participants aren't *ready* to ask questions. The strategies that follow will help you to change these dynamics. Participants will be more prepared to compose questions because they have had a chance to think over the material.

41 Learning Starts with a Question

```
┌─────────────────── Overview ───────────────────┐
│ The process of learning something new is more effective │
│ if the learner is in an active, searching mode rather than │
│ a passive mode. One way to create the active-learning │
│ mode is to stimulate participants to delve into subject │
│ matter on their own without prior explanation from you. │
│ This simple strategy stimulates question asking, the key │
│ to learning. │
└─────────────────────────────────────────────────┘
```

Procedure

1. Distribute to participants an instructional handout of your own choosing. Key to your choice of handouts is the need to stimulate questions from the participants. A handout that provides broad information but lacks details or explanatory backup material is ideal. An interesting chart or diagram that illustrates some knowledge is a good choice. A text that is open to interpretation is another good choice. The goal is to evoke curiosity.

2. Ask participants to study the handout with a partner. Request that the partners make as much sense of the handout as possible and that they place question marks next to information they do not understand. Encourage participants to insert as many question marks as they wish. If time permits, form the pairs into quartets and allow time for each pair to help the other.

3. Reconvene the group and answer participants' questions. In essence, your session will be directed by the group's questions rather than by a preset plan. Or if you wish, listen to all the questions first and then proceed with a preset plan, making a special effort to respond to the questions posed by participants.

Variations

1. If you feel that participants will be lost trying to study the material entirely on their own, provide some additional information to help guide them in their inquiries. Then, proceed with the study groups.

2. Begin the procedure with individual study rather than partner study.

Case Example

In a course on process improvement, the trainer distributes a flow chart that depicts the steps for washing a car. The trainer asks the participants to study the chart with a learning partner and to place question marks at any point in the diagram that is not clear to them.

HOW TO WASH A CAR

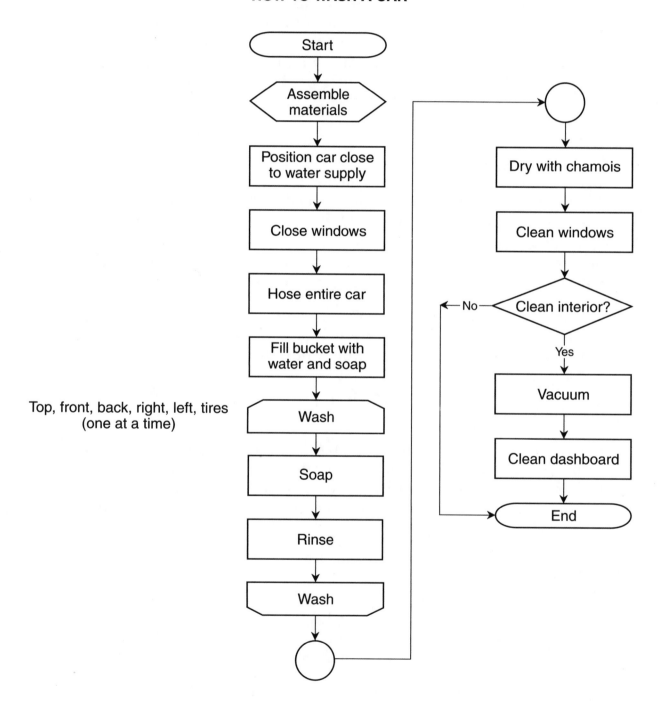

Top, front, back, right, left, tires (one at a time)

101 Ways to Make Training Active

In the ensuing discussion, the participants ask the following questions:

- What do the different shapes mean?
- What do the empty circles mean?
- What is the side annotation?
- Why are there two "wash" shapes?

42 **Planted Questions**

Overview

This technique enables you to present information in response to questions that have been "planted" with selected participants. Although you are, in effect, giving a well-prepared lesson, it appears to other participants that you are merely conducting a question-and-answer session.

Procedure

1. Choose three to six questions that will guide your lesson and sequence them logically.

2. Write each of the questions on an index card along with the cue you will use to signal a participant to ask that question. Cues you might use include the following:

   - scratching your nose
   - taking off your eyeglasses
   - snapping your fingers
   - yawning

3. Prior to the session, select the participants who will ask the questions. Give each an index card and explain the cue. Make sure the participants do not reveal to anyone else that they are "plants."

4. Open the question-and-answer session by announcing the topic and giving your first cue. Call on the first "plant," answer the question, and then continue with the rest of the cues and questions.

5. Now open the floor to new questions. You should see several hands go up.

This technique was created by Rebecca Birch and Cynthia Denton-Ade.

Variations

1. Have the answers to the questions already prepared on flip charts, overhead transparencies, or instructional handouts. Dramatically reveal the answer to each question.

2. Give the planted questions to your most uninterested or hostile participants.

Case Example

In a leadership training session, the trainer briefly discusses the characteristics of an effective leader and then opens the floor for questions. During a previous break, the trainer had given each of four participants one of the following questions on an instruction card:

- What is the difference between a leader and a manager?
- Why is this leadership "stuff" such a big deal?
- How can you teach someone to be a leader?
- Does someone have to have all those characteristics in order to be effective?

The following is a sample of one of the instruction cards:

DO NOT SHOW THIS CARD TO ANYONE.

When our break is over, I'm going to be discussing characteristics of an effective leader and ask if there are any questions. When I *scratch my nose,* raise your hand and ask the following question:

*What is the difference between a leader
and a manager?*

Do not read the question directly from the card. Memorize it or say it in your own words.

---

43 | Role Reversal Questions

Overview

Even if you ask participants to be thinking of questions throughout a session, not just at the end, you may still get a lukewarm response when you ask "Are there any questions?" With this technique, you reverse roles: You ask questions and the participants try to respond.

Procedure

1. Compose questions you would raise about some learning material *if you were a participant*. Create questions that do the following:

   - seek to clarify difficult or complex material (for example, "Would you explain again the process for creating a customer refund?")

   - compare the material to other information (for example, "How is this method different from the process followed by Division B?")

   - challenge specific points of view in the lecture material (for example, "Why is it necessary to revise the process? Wouldn't that lead to a lot of confusion?")

   - request examples of the ideas being discussed (for example, "Could you give me an example of how to write a disciplinary letter?")

   - test the applicability of the material (for example, "How could I use this idea in this organization?")

2. At the beginning of a question period, announce to the participants that you are going to "be" them, and they collectively are going to "be" you. Proceed to ask your questions.

3. Be argumentative, humorous, and whatever else it takes to get the participants to overcome their hesitation and bombard you with answers.

4. Reversing roles a few times will keep your participants alert and prompt them to ask questions on their own.

This technique was developed by Linc Fisch.

101 Ways to Make Training Active

Variations

1. Instead of employing this technique at the start of a question-and-answer session, use it when participants have become complacent about asking questions.

2. Turn the event into a "media conference." You become the media, introducing yourself as "Chris from CNN" or the like, and press the class with questions that probe, attack, or mock the learning material.

Case Example

In a course for managers on conducting effective meetings, the instructor assumes the role of a participant and asks the following questions of the group:

- Why should I have an agenda? Doesn't an agenda make a meeting formal and stuffy?
- How can I start a meeting on time when key people aren't there?
- How can I encourage more participation?
- What do I do about the person who wants to monopolize the discussion?
- Would you explain what "gatekeeping" means?

TEAM LEARNING

One of the best ways to promote active learning is to give learning assignments to be carried out in small teams. The peer support and diversity of viewpoints, knowledge, and skills help make team learning a valuable part of active training. However, team learning is not always effective. There may be unequal participation, poor communication, and confusion instead of real learning. The strategies that follow are designed to maximize the benefits of team learning and to minimize the pitfalls.

44 Information Search

┌─────────────── **Overview** ───────────────┐

This method can be likened to an open-book test. Teams search for information (normally covered in a lecture) that answers questions posed to them. This method is especially helpful in livening up dry material.

└──┘

Procedure

1. Create a group of questions for which the answers can be found in resource material you have made available for participants. The resource material can include the following:

   - handouts
   - documents
   - textbooks
   - reference guides
   - computer-accessed information
   - artifacts
   - "hard" equipment

2. Hand out the questions about the topic.

3. Form participants into small teams and have them search for the answers. A friendly competition can be set up to encourage participation.

4. Reconvene the group and review answers. Expand on the answers to enlarge the scope of learning.

Variations

1. Word your questions so that participants must *infer* answers from the resource materials rather than obtain the answers directly from the material.

2. Instead of asking participants to hunt for answers to questions, assign a different task such as a case problem to solve, an exercise in which participants have to match items, or a set of scrambled words which, if unscrambled, denote important terms contained in the resource information.

Case Example

Participants training to be claims adjusters are given the following report from a medical doctor:

> Mr. Smith sustained fractures of L4 and L5 vertebral bodies on 1/20 when he was involved in a motor vehicle accident while wearing a seat belt. There was no loss of consciousness. He complained of severe back pain and was seen in orthopedic consultation on 1/20 at the request of his physician, Dr. Christopher White.
>
> On examination at that time he had tenderness in the lumbar region with moderately severe paraspinal spasm in the lumbar region. There was full range of motion of both hips, no lower extremity neurological deficits. Straight leg raise was equivocal at 45 degrees bilaterally. X-rays disclosed 10-15% anterior compression fractures L4 and L5 vertebrae without retro or spondylolisthesis. He was advised bed rest, traction, warm soaks, and progressive ambulation and physiotherapy. We followed him closely until his discharge.
>
> He returned to the office on 2/12. Range of motion was 0-45 degrees, slightly crouching antalgic gait, straight leg raise was equivocal at 60 degrees bilaterally with hamstring tightness. There were no lower extremity neurological deficits.
>
> Lumbosacral spine films, including flexion extension films, revealed no spondyloretrolisthesis or instability at the fracture level.
>
> I recommended he return to full duty 3/1, anticipate gradual healing of the fractures over the next several months and return here in 3 weeks for follow-up.

Accompanying the letter are the following instructions:

Using the resource materials available to your team, answer the following questions about the attached physician's report. Be as specific as possible in answering.

1. Where is the injury located? What are the findings of the examination?

2. What type of fractures were sustained? Describe.

3. What is spondylolisthesis? Spondyloretrolisthesis?

4. Why does the report mention neurological deficits?

45 The Study Group

Overview

This method gives participants the responsibility to study
learning material and to clarify its content as a group
without the trainer's presence. The assignment needs to
be specific enough so that the resulting study session will
be effective and the group able to be self-managing.

Procedure

1. Give participants a short, well-formatted handout covering lecture material, a brief text, or an interesting chart or diagram. Ask them to review it silently. The study group will work best when the material is moderately challenging or open to widespread interpretation.

2. Form subgroups and give them a quiet space to conduct their study sessions.

3. Provide clear instructions that guide participants to study and explicate the material carefully. Include directions such as the following:

   - **Clarify** the content.

   - **Create** examples, illustrations, or applications of the information or ideas.

   - **Identify** points that are confusing or with which you disagree.

   - **Argue** with the text; develop an opposing point of view.

   - **Assess** how well you understand the material.

4. Assign jobs such as facilitator, timekeeper, recorder, or spokesperson to subgroup members. (See "Ten Alternatives for Selecting Group Leaders and Filling Other Jobs," page 25.)

5. Reconvene the entire group and do one or more of the following:

   - Review the material together.

   - Quiz participants.

   - Obtain questions.

- Ask participants to assess how well they understand the material.
- Provide an application exercise for participants to solve.

Variations

1. Do not form subgroups. Create a full-class study group. Read the material aloud. Stop the reading to answer participants' questions, to pose questions of your own, or to expound on the text.

2. If the group is large enough, create four or six study groups. Then combine pairs of study groups and ask them to compare notes and help one another.

Case Example

In a course on project management, the trainer addresses the question "What makes project management successful?"

The trainer provides the following handout and asks participants to form subgroups to study the material. The subgroups are asked to discuss each concept to clarify the content, create an example, and assess how well they understand the material. They are also asked to identify the points that they find confusing.

What Makes Project Management Successful?

1. Successful project management is the result of establishing and communicating clear goals and schedules. Goals must meet the following SMART criteria:

   - **Specific:** Write the goals so that they express exactly what you are going to accomplish.

   - **Measurable:** Identify the deliverables.

   - **Agreed on:** Use a consensus-seeking process to ensure agreement by all those involved in the project.

   - **Realistic:** Make sure that you have the appropriate resources to successfully complete the project.

   - **Time-bound:** Set deadlines and target completion dates.

   Discuss this item.

Give an example.

How well do you understand this idea?   1   2   3   4   5
                                        not well   very well

2. Winning project managers are proactive. They are constantly evaluating: What is likely to go wrong? How and when will I know? What will I do about it? How will I do it?

Discuss this item.
Give an example.

How well do you understand this idea?   1   2   3   4   5
                                          not well   very well

3. Successful projects are the result of successful project teams. Some characteristics of a successful team are that roles are clearly defined; conflicts are resolved openly and quickly; each team member's contribution is valued; communication is frequent and open; and there is a high level of interdependency among team members.

Discuss this item.
Give an example.

How well do you understand this idea?   1   2   3   4   5
                                          not well   very well

46 Card Sort

┌─────────────── **Overview** ───────────────┐

This is an active team-based strategy that can be used to teach concepts, classification characteristics, or product knowledge or to review information. The physical movement featured can help to energize a tired group.

└──┘

Procedure

1. Give each participant an index card that contains information or an example that fits into one or more categories. The following are some sample categories:

   - team "task" behaviors vs. team "maintenance" behaviors
   - functions of various departments in an organization
   - behaviors that illustrate the needs for achievement, affiliation, and power
   - symptoms of different illnesses
   - information that fits into varied parts of a job résumé

2. Ask participants to mill around the room and find others whose cards fit the same category. (You may announce the categories beforehand or allow the participants to discover them.)

3. Have participants with same-category cards present themselves to the rest of the group.

4. As each category is presented, make any teaching points you think are important.

Variations

1. Ask each group to make a teaching presentation about its category.

2. At the beginning of the activity, form teams. Give each team a complete set of cards. Be sure the cards are shuffled so that the categories they are

to be sorted into are not obvious. Ask each team to sort the cards. Each team can obtain a score for the number of cards sorted correctly.

Case Example

Special-education teachers are divided into two teams. Each team is given a shuffled deck of cards containing the trade names of medications prescribed, at times, for the children in its classrooms. Both teams are to sort the cards into two even piles: one of sedatives and the other of stimulants.
   The following is the correct sorting:

Sedatives:

Atarax®
Noctec®
Doriden®
Quaalude®
Amytal®
Benadryl®

Stimulants:

Deaner®
Dexedrine®
Cylert®
Ritalin®
Benzedrine®
Desoxyn®

47 **Learning Tournament**

Overview

This technique combines a study group with team competition. It can be used to promote the learning of a wide variety of facts, concepts, and even skills.

Procedure

1. Divide participants into teams with two to eight members. Make sure the teams have an equal number of members. (If this cannot be done, you will have to average each team's score.)

2. Provide the teams with material to study together such as lecture notes, a brief text, or an interesting chart or diagram.

3. Develop several questions that test comprehension of the learning material. Use formats that make self-scoring easy, such as multiple choice, fill in the blanks, true/false, or terms to define.

4. Give a portion of the questions to participants. Refer to this as Round 1 of the learning tournament. **Each participant must answer the questions individually.**

5. After the participants have completed the questions, provide the answers and ask participants to count the number of questions they answered correctly. Then, have them pool their scores with every other member of their team to obtain a team score. Announce the scores of each team.

6. Ask the teams to study again for the second round of the tournament. Then ask more questions as part of Round 2. Have teams once again pool their scores and add them to their Round 1 scores.

7. You can have as many rounds as you like, but be sure to allow the teams a study session between each round.

This strategy was created by Sivasailam Thiagarajan ("Thiagi").

Variations

1. Penalize participants for wrong answers by assigning a score of -2 or -3. If a question is left unanswered, the blank should be scored as 0.

2. Make the performance of a series of skills the basis of the tournament.

Case Example

In a course on human-resource management, the trainer distributes information about the Americans with Disabilities Act and asks teams to study it. In the first round of the learning tournament, every participant takes a true/false test. The following five statements are given:

1. Any new building over two stories high must have an elevator.

2. Organizations with fewer than seventy-five employees are exempt from compliance.

3. Physical requirements for a job may be listed in the job description.

4. The cost of retraining a newly disabled employee is completely assumed by the employer.

5. The term "reasonable accommodation" is clearly defined by government regulations.

After the answers are reviewed by the trainer, the participants total their individual scores to obtain a team score. Round 1 is now over and each team returns to study the information further to prepare for Round 2 of the tournament.

48 The Power of Two

┌─────────────────── **Overview** ───────────────────┐

This activity is used to promote cooperative learning and
to reinforce the importance and benefits of synergy, that
is, that two heads are indeed better than one.

└──┘

Procedure

1. List topic-related questions on a flip chart, transparency, or chalkboard
   or in participant workbooks.

2. Ask participants to answer the questions individually.

3. After all participants have completed their answers, ask the participants
   to form pairs. Members of each pair share their answers with each other.

4. Ask the pairs to create a new answer to each question, improving on
   each individual's response.

5. When all pairs have written new answers, compare the answers of each
   pair to the others in the group.

Variations

1. Invite the entire group to select the best answer for each question.

2. To save time, assign specific questions to each pair rather than having all
   pairs answer all of the questions.

Case Example

In a session on creative problem solving, the trainer writes the following questions on the flip chart:

- What is creativity?
- Why is creative problem solving an important skill?

- What are some traits of the best problem solvers?
- What are the barriers to creative problem solving?
- What are some tools and techniques to stretch thinking and unleash creativity?

Participants each write responses to the questions and then compare answers with their partners. New answers are then developed collaboratively.

49 Team Quiz

```
┌─────────────────────── Overview ───────────────────────┐
│                                                         │
│  This team technique is an enjoyable and nonthreatening │
│  way to increase the participants' accountability for   │
│  what they are learning.                                │
│                                                         │
└─────────────────────────────────────────────────────────┘
```

Procedure

1. Choose a topic that can be presented in three segments.

2. Divide the participants into three teams.

3. Explain the format of the session and start the presentation. Limit it to ten minutes or less.

4. Have Team A prepare a short-answer quiz based on the first segment of the lecture. The quiz should take no more than five minutes to prepare. Teams B and C use this time to review their notes.

5. Team A quizzes a member of Team B. If Team B cannot answer the question, Team C gets an opportunity to answer the same question.

6. Team A directs its next question to a member of Team C and repeats the process. Team A continues asking questions until the quiz is complete.

7. When the quiz is over, continue with the second segment of your lesson, and appoint Team B as quizmaster.

8. After Team B completes its quiz, continue with the third segment of your lesson, and appoint Team C as quizmaster.

Variations

1. Give teams prepared quiz questions from which they select when it is their turn to be the quizmaster.

This technique was created by Rebecca Birch and Cynthia Denton-Ade.

2. Conduct one continuous lesson. Divide participants into two teams. At the end of the lesson, have the two teams quiz each other.

Case Example

In a communication skills workshop, the trainer divides the group into two teams to prepare questions on two different sections of the lesson as follows:

Team A develops the following questions about *sending communication*:

- What is an example of an "I" message?
- How much impact does nonverbal communication have in the messages we send?
- How could you say "You have to complete this assignment" in a more tactful manner?

Team B develops the following questions about *receiving communication*:

- What else can you say to confirm what you heard other than "What I hear you saying is..."?
- How many times faster can a person listen than talk?
- What is "perception checking"?

PEER TEACHING

Some experts believe that a subject is truly mastered when a learner is able to teach it to someone else. Peer teaching gives participants the opportunity to learn something well and at the same time to become resources for one another. The strategies that follow are practical ways to involve peer teaching in a training context. They also allow the trainer to supplement, when necessary, the teaching done by participants.

50 Group-to-Group Exchange

Overview

In this strategy, different assignments are given to different subgroups of participants. Each subgroup then "teaches" what it has learned to the rest of the group. This activity promotes a spirited exchange of views about any topic for which there are differing ideas, positions, concepts, or approaches.

Procedure

1. Select a topic that promotes an exchange of views (as opposed to a debate). Examples of topics include the following:

   - two approaches to closing a sale
   - different ways to improve employee performance
   - project-management methods
   - the ideas of two or more writers

2. Divide the participants into as many subgroups as there are positions for the topic. In most cases, two to four subgroups are appropriate for this activity. Provide each subgroup with appropriate background information on the selected topic. Give each subgroup up to thirty minutes to create a presentation for the assigned topic viewpoint. For example, if the topic is leadership, one subgroup might present Hersey and Blanchard's[1] concepts about Situational Leadership™ and a second subgroup might present Lewin's[2] studies of "autocratic, democratic, and laissez-faire leaders."

3. When the preparation phase is completed, ask each subgroup to select a spokesperson. Invite each spokesperson to address the other subgroup(s).

---

[1] *Management of Organizational Behaviors* by P. Hersey & K. Blanchard, Englewood Cliffs, NJ: Prentice-Hall, 1977.

[2] *Field Theory in Social Science* by K. Lewin, New York: Harper, 1951.

4. After a brief presentation, encourage participants to ask questions of the presenter or to offer their own views. Allow other members of the spokesperson's subgroup to respond.

5. Continue the remaining presentations until each subgroup has expressed its views and has responded to audience questions and comments. Then, compare and contrast the views that were exchanged.

Variations

1. Allow a considerably longer period of preparation. Ask subgroups to do extensive research before their presentations.

2. Use a panel or fishbowl discussion format for each of the subgroups' presentations.

Case Example

The trainer for a session on dealing with conflict divides the participants into three subgroups to address the following three conflict-management styles:

- Cooperative: Seeks a win/win solution; approaches the problem as a collaborative effort.

- Competitive: Sees conflict as a win/lose situation; tends to attack the other position and seeks to win at all costs.

- Avoidance: Pretends that conflict does not exist or that, if ignored, it will eventually go away; uncomfortable with any kind of confrontation.

Each subgroup is asked to study the characteristics of its assigned style and to make a presentation to the rest of the group. Following this, the entire group discusses the three styles.

51 Jigsaw Learning

Overview

Jigsaw learning is similar to group-to-group exchange
with one important difference: Every single participant
teaches something. It is an exciting alternative whenever
there is material to be learned that can be segmented or
"chunked" and where no one segment must be taught before the others. Each participant learns something that,
when combined with the material learned by others,
forms a coherent body of knowledge.

Procedure

1. Choose learning material that can be broken into segments. A segment
   can be as short as one sentence or as long as several pages. (If the material is lengthy, ask participants to read their assignments before the
   session.)
   Examples of appropriate material include the following:

   - a multi-point handout (for example, "Ten Strategies for Forming
     Groups," page 23)
   - a text that has different sections or subheadings
   - a list of definitions
   - a group of magazine-length articles or other kinds of short reading
     material

2. Count the number of learning segments and the number of participants.
   In an equitable manner, give out different assignments to different subgroups. For example, imagine a class of twelve participants. Assume that
   you can divide learning materials into three segments or "chunks." You
   might then be able to form quartets, assigning each group either segment 1, 2, or 3. Then ask each quartet or "study group" to read, discuss,
   and learn the material assigned to them. (If you wish, you can form pairs
   or "study buddies" first and then combine the pairs into quartets.)

3. After the study period, form "cooperative learning" subgroups. Such subgroups contain a representative of every study group in the class. In the example just given, the members of each quartet could count off 1, 2, 3, and 4. Form cooperative learning subgroups of participants with the same number. The result will be four trios. In each trio will be one person who has studied segment 1, one who has studied segment 2, and one who has studied segment 3. The following diagram displays this sequence.[1]

Total Group Explanation

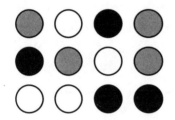

Study Group

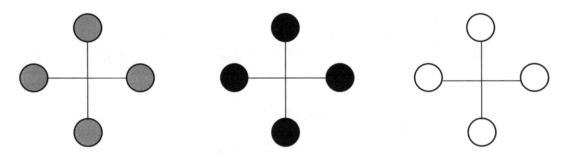

Cooperative Learning Groups

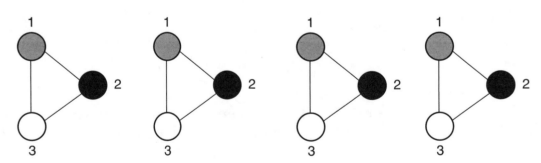

---

[1] Diagram reproduced from *20 Active Training Programs, Vol. II* by M. Silberman, S. Jullierat, K. Lawson, & N.C. Lewine. Copyright © 1994 by Pfeiffer & Company, San Diego, CA.

101 Ways to Make Training Active

4. Ask the members of the cooperative learning subgroups to teach one another what they have learned.

5. Reconvene the full group for review and to answer remaining questions to ensure accurate understanding.

Variations

1. In many instances, the number of participants cannot be divided evenly into the number of learning segments. If this is the case, you can adjust by using learning partners instead of subgroups. Divide the learning material into only two segments, assigning one segment to one member of a pair and the other segment to his or her partner. For example, in a seven-point handout, one person can be assigned points 1 through 4 and the partner can be assigned points 5 through 7. Create "study buddies" of pair members with the same assignment. Then have the original pairs meet again to teach one another what they have studied.

2. Assign to different participants the responsibility for learning a skill rather than cognitive information. Have participants teach one another the skills they have learned.

Case Example

A class on business development deals with the types of legal structures for a business.

The instructor creates handouts describing each of the following entities:

- S Corporation
- C Corporation
- Partnership
- Sole Proprietorship
- Limited Partnership

Five study groups are formed and each group is given one of the entities to study and be able to explain to someone else.

Groups are then reconfigured to include one member from each of the study groups. Each person then teaches the others about the business entity that he or she studied, pointing out key features as well as benefits and drawbacks.

52 Everyone Is a Teacher Here

┌─────────────────── **Overview** ───────────────────┐

This is an easy strategy for obtaining class-wide participation and individual accountability. It gives every participant the opportunity to act as a "teacher" for other participants.

└──┘

Procedure

1. Hand out an index card to each participant. Ask participants to write down a question they have about the learning material being studied in the training or a specific topic they would like discussed.

2. Collect the cards, shuffle them, and distribute one of them to each participant. Ask the participants to read silently the question or topic on their card and think of a response.

3. Invite volunteers to read aloud the card they received and to give a response.

4. After a response is given, ask the others in the group to add to what the volunteer has contributed.

5. Continue as long as there are volunteers.

Variations

1. Hold on to the cards you collect. Create a panel of respondents. Read each card and ask for discussion from the panelists. Rotate the members of the panel frequently.

2. Ask participants to write down on cards an opinion or observation they have about the learning material. Ask for volunteers to share their comments, and have other participants agree or disagree with the opinions or observations offered.

Case Example

In a session on retirement planning, participants have read material on retirement-planning options. Some of the questions raised by the participants follow:

- How soon should a person begin to plan for retirement?
- What is the difference between an IRA and an SEP?
- How much should someone save per month for retirement?
- What are annuities?
- What kind of investment mix should a retired person have?

The instructor follows the procedure given above, allowing participants to respond to one anothers' questions.

53 | Peer Lessons

Overview

This is a strategy to promote peer teaching that places the entire responsibility for teaching fellow participants on the group members.

Procedure

1. Divide the participants into subgroups. Create as many subgroups as you have topics to be taught.

2. Give each subgroup some information, a concept, or a skill to teach others. The following are some sample topics:

   - the structure of an effective paragraph
   - how to become a better listener
   - conducting performance appraisals of employees
   - how to negotiate a win-win agreement

3. Ask each subgroup to design a way to present or teach its topic to the rest of the participants. Advise the subgroups to avoid a lecture presentation and to try to make the learning experience as active as possible for participants.

4. Suggest that subgroups consider any of the following methods:

   - visual aids
   - a demonstration skit
   - examples and/or analogies
   - involvement through discussion, quiz games, writing tasks, role playing, mental imagery, or case study
   - questions and answers

   You might also suggest some methods from *101 Ways to Make Training Active* as teaching strategies.

5. Allow sufficient time for planning and preparation (either during or outside of the session). Then, have each subgroup present its lesson. Applaud the effort of each subgroup.

Variations

1. Instead of subgroup teaching, have participants teach others individually or in small groups.

2. Allow subgroups to ask participants to complete a reading assignment before the presentations.

Case Example ━━━━━━━━━━━━━━━━━━━━━━━━

In a course on career planning, the trainer divides the group into five subgroups and assigns each subgroup one of the following topics:

- assessing your skills and accomplishments
- networking skills
- preparing a résumé
- job-hunting resources
- polishing your interview skills

The subgroups present their topics as follows:

- The subgroup assigned to the topic of skills assessment prepares a self-assessment questionnaire and asks participants to complete it during the session.

- The networking-skills subgroup presents its content points through a panel discussion during which panel members share personal experiences and techniques they have used in developing networking skills.

- The subgroup presenting the résumé collects examples of good and poor résumés for the group to analyze.

- To convey the wide array of job-hunting resources available, the subgroup assigned this topic prepares a crossword puzzle for the group to complete.

- The interview-skills subgroup presents a skit demonstrating the do's and don'ts of interviewing.

54 Participant-Created Case Studies

┌─────────────────── **Overview** ───────────────────┐

Case study is widely heralded as one of the best learning methods. A typical case discussion focuses on the issues involved in a concrete situation or example, the action that should be taken and the lessons that can be learned, and the ways of handling or avoiding such situations in the future. The technique that follows allows participants to create their own case studies.

└──┘

Procedure

1. Divide the participants into pairs or trios. Invite them to develop a case study that the remainder of the group can analyze and discuss.

2. Indicate that the purpose of a case study is to learn about a topic by examining a concrete situation or example that reflects that topic. Provide some of the following examples:

   - A transcript of a performance review can be analyzed to study how to appraise employees effectively.

   - An account of how a company set up a succession planning program can be used to study promotion policies.

   - A dialogue between a manager and an employee can be examined to learn how to provide positive reinforcement.

   - The steps taken by management in a company undergoing a merger can be studied to learn about organizational change.

3. Provide adequate time for the pairs or trios to develop a short case situation (100 to 200 words long) that poses an issue to be discussed or a problem to be solved that is relevant to the subject matter of the session. Give the participants the following guidelines:

   - The case study can be a real example or an invented one.

   - Make the material subtle and challenging; do not be obvious about what is right or wrong.

- Allow for different points of view.

4. When the case studies are complete, have the subgroups present them to the participants. Allow a member of the subgroup to lead the case discussion.

Variations

1. Obtain a small number of volunteers who prepare case studies in advance for the rest of the participants. (The preparation of a case study is an excellent learning assignment.)

2. Create an even number of subgroups. Pair up subgroups and have them exchange case studies.

Case Example

In a session on sexual harassment, four subgroups develop the following case studies:

1. Lois worked in a shipyard as a welder. Pictures of nude and partially nude women were posted throughout the building. There was graffiti on the walls with suggestive messages for various people. Male employees and supervisors made off-color remarks to Lois and also said to her, "There's nothing worse than having to work around women."

2. John was head of a military EEO office. He frequently said things to one of his female staff members like "Okay, babe" and "Listen here, woman." He would yell at her for leaving the office and even try to prevent her from leaving by blocking the doorway. John once complained to a fellow manager that he had "dumb females working for him who couldn't read or write."

3. Margaret wanted a promotion that was given to Donna. Everyone in the office knew that Donna had an affair with the male supervisor who granted the promotion. The supervisor would call female subordinates while they were at work and brag about sexual experiences he had had with several female workers. He even mentioned to Margaret that Donna would get the promotion because she was "very good at making him feel good."

4. Susan had been having an affair with her boss for approximately two years. She had always been interested in him and had jumped at the opportunity to become his secretary when the position became available. She initiated the relationship by making suggestive comments and inviting him to dinner. When Susan tried to end the relationship, her boss became quite upset and begged her not to end it. She broke it off anyway. She then began to get negative performance appraisals and was written up for minor infractions. She finally quit because of the continuous criticism of her performance.

A spokesperson from each subgroup conducts a discussion of each case. The questions fall into the following categories:

- Discussion starters: "Is this sexual harassment? Why or why not?"

- Probing and challenging questions: "What sexual harassment guidelines apply in this case?"

- Application questions: "How does this impact the workplace?"

- Predictive and hypothetical questions: "If you were the 'victim' what would you do?"

- Analytical and evaluative questions: "Which part of the case scenario was most damaging?"

- Summary questions: "How does this relate to your role as a manager?"

55 In the News

Overview

This activity is an interesting way of getting participants involved and arousing their interest in the topic even before they attend the session. This peer teaching approach will also result in a wealth of material and information that can be shared with all participants.

Procedure

1. Ask participants to bring to the session articles, news items, editorials, and cartoons related to the training topic.

2. Divide the group into subgroups and ask members of each subgroup to share their items with one another and to choose the two or three most interesting items.

3. Reconvene the entire group and ask representatives from each subgroup to share their choices with the entire group.

4. As the representatives are reporting, listen for important points that you intend to address in the session and use that information to promote discussion.

Variations

1. Collect and copy all the items and distribute them to the participants as a follow-up to the training. Or ask participants to submit their items prior to the first session. Copy the items and send them to participants to be read before the training.

2. Use the news items as case studies or as the basis of role plays.

Case Example

In a session on safety training, participants are asked to bring in newspaper articles about various accidents. For example, one recent article recounted the death of a zookeeper who had not taken the proper precautions before entering the area occupied by a white tiger. Another example was of an industrial accident that occurred when an employee was not wearing safety gear. After the subgroups have had an opportunity to share their articles with one another, the trainer conducts a full-group discussion during which the group identifies the common link in all the stories and then begins to discuss the safety procedures and issues in their own organization.

56 Poster Session

Overview

This alternative presentation method is an excellent way to capture the imagination, invite an exchange of ideas, and briefly inform participants. This technique is also a novel and graphic way of enabling participants to express their perceptions and feelings about the topic in a nonthreatening environment.

Procedure

1. Each participant selects a topic related to the general topic of the training.

2. Each participant prepares a visual display of his or her concept on poster board or a flip chart. (You will determine the size.) The poster display should be self-explanatory, that is, observers should easily understand the idea without any further written or oral explanation. However, participants may choose to accompany the poster with a one-page handout offering more detail and serving as further reference material.

3. During the designated session, participants post their visual presentations and freely circulate around the room viewing and discussing one anothers' posters.

4. Fifteen minutes prior to the end of the session, convene all the participants and discuss what they found valuable about the activity.

Variation

1. Form teams of two or three participants instead of making individual assignments, particularly if the topic is limited in scope.

2. Follow up a poster session with a panel discussion, using some displayers as panelists.

Case Example

In a training program on stress management, subtopics that are assigned include the following:

- causes of stress
- symptoms of stress
- effects of stress on self and others
- stress reducers

One of the participants illustrates the symptoms of stress by creating a poster display that shows the following pictures:

- an overweight person on a scale
- someone drinking an alcoholic drink
- two people arguing
- a person with a headache

Below each picture is a short paragraph explaining how and why a stressed person might be exhibiting the symptom portrayed.

INDEPENDENT LEARNING

Full-group and team learning can be
enhanced by independent-learning
activities. When participants learn on
their own, they can focus and reflect.
They also have the opportunity to take
personal responsibility for their learning.
The strategies that follow are a combin-
ation of techniques that can be used
inside and outside the training session.

57 Imagine

┌─────────────── **Overview** ───────────────┐

Through visual imagery, participants can develop their own plans and ideas. This technique is effective as a creative supplement to team learning. It can also serve as a springboard to an independent project that may initially seem overwhelming to participants.

└──┘

Procedure

1. Introduce the topic that will be covered. Explain to participants that the subject requires creativity and that the use of visual imagery may assist their efforts.

2. Instruct the participants to close their eyes. Introduce a relaxation activity that will clear current thoughts from the participants' minds. Use background music, dimmed lights, and measured breathing to achieve results.

3. Then ask participants, with their eyes still closed, to try to visualize sights and sounds such as a rosebud, their bedrooms, a changing traffic light, or the patter of rain.

4. When group members are relaxed, provide an image for them to build on. You might suggest any of the following:

   - a future experience
   - an unfamiliar setting
   - a problem to solve
   - an on-the-job success
   - an ideal place to work

5. As the image is described, provide regular silent intervals so that participants can build their own visual image. Build in questions that encourage the use of all senses:

   - What does the image look like?
   - Who do you see? What are they doing?

- How do you feel?

6. Conclude guiding the image and instruct group members to remember their images. Slowly end the activity.

7. Ask the participants to form small groups and to share their imagery experiences. Ask them to describe to one another the images, using as many senses as possible.

Variations

1. Now that participants have "rehearsed" in their minds how they would act in a specific situation, invite them to plan out how they might actually implement their thoughts when back on the job.

2. Conduct an imagery activity in which participants experience failure. Then, have them imagine a success.

Case Example

A trainer for a session on job-search strategies helps the participants prepare for job interviews.

1. The trainer takes the participants through a series of relaxation activities.

2. While in a relaxed state, participants are then asked by the trainer to imagine themselves sitting in an office with a job interviewer.

3. The trainer asks the participants to keep their eyes closed and to continue to breathe deeply while she asks the following questions:

- What are you wearing?
- What time of day is it?
- What does the office look like?
- Is it dark or light in the office?
- What kind of chair are you sitting on?
- Where is the interviewer sitting?
- What does the interviewer look like?
- How do you feel?

4. At the end of the activity, the participants discuss how they felt during the imagery experience and what they can do to make the actual interview a pleasant experience.

58 Writing in the Here and Now

┌─────────────────── **Overview** ───────────────────┐

Writing allows participants to reflect on experiences they have had. A dramatic way to promote independent reflection is to ask participants to write a *present-tense* action account of an experience they have had (as if it were happening in the "here and now").

└──┘

Procedure

1. Select the kind of experience (such as a work-related incident) you want participants to write about. It can be a past or future event. Among the possible events are the following:

   ■ a recent conflict situation

   ■ a team meeting

   ■ an incidence of coaching an employee

   ■ a first day on a new job

   ■ a performance review

   ■ a presentation

   ■ an incident with a client or customer

   ■ a training session

2. Inform participants about the experience you have selected for the purpose of reflective writing. Tell them that a valuable way to reflect on the experience is to relive it or experience it for the first time in the "here and now." By doing so, the impact is clearer and more dramatic than writing about something in the "there and then" or in the "distant future."

3. Provide a firm surface for participants to write on. Establish privacy and quiet.

4. Ask participants to write, in the present tense, about the experience selected. Have them begin at the start of the experience and write what

they and others are doing and feeling, such as "I am standing before a group of managers doing my first sales presentation. I find it hard to believe that I am actually doing this!" Invite participants to write as much as they wish about the events that occur and the feelings that are generated.

5. Allow the participants ample writing time; they should not feel rushed. When they are finished, invite them to review their reflections.

6. Discuss what new actions the participants might undertake in the future.

Variations

1. To help participants get in the mood for reflective writing, first conduct a mental-imagery activity or hold a group discussion relevant to the topic you are assigning.

2. Ask participants to share what they have written. One option is to invite a limited number of volunteers to read their finished work. A second option is to assign partners and have them share their writing with each other.

Case Example

In a program on organizational vision, the trainer asks participants to think about how their unit would be functioning eighteen months from now if anything were possible. They are asked to imagine the following:

- the unique contribution the unit is making to the company
- how the unit is perceived by other units in the company
- the effective ways people in the unit are relating to one another
- how much fun people are having because they are a part of the unit

Participants are then asked to write about this vision as if it were true now. The participants use phrases such as "We are creating new approaches to customer service all the time."

59 Mindmaps

Overview

Mindmapping is a creative way for individual participants to generate ideas, record learning, begin a new project, or evaluate an existing project. Asking participants to create a mindmap during a training session enables them to identify clearly and creatively what they have learned or what they are planning.

Procedure

1. Select the topic for mindmapping. Some possibilities include the following:

   - a problem or issue about which you want participants to create action ideas

   - a concept or skill you have just taught

   - a project to be planned by the participants

2. Construct for the group a simple mindmap using colors, images, or symbols. One example would be a trip to the grocery store during which a person shops from a mindmap that categorizes items needed according to the departments in which they are found (for example, dairy, produce, and frozen foods). Explain how the colors, images, and symbols in your mindmap promote whole-brain thinking (versus right brain/left brain thinking). Invite participants to cite simple examples of activities from their daily lives that they could mindmap.

3. Provide paper, marking pens, and any other resources you think will help participants to create colorful, graphic mindmaps. Give participants the mindmapping assignment. Suggest that they begin their maps by creating a pictorial center, depicting the topic or main idea. Then, encourage the participants to break the whole into smaller components and to depict these components around the periphery of the map (using color and graphics). **Urge them to represent each idea pictorially, using as few**

words as possible. Following this, they can elaborate as details pop into their minds.

4. Allow plenty of time for participants to develop their mindmaps. Encourage them to look at other people's work to stimulate ideas.

5. Ask participants to share their mindmaps. Conduct a discussion about the value of this creative way to outline ideas.

Variations

1. Assign a team mindmap instead of having the participants work on an individual basis.

2. Use computers to generate mindmaps.

Case Example

In a session on business writing, the instructor divides the group into teams of four and asks each team to create a mindmap in preparation for a proposal requesting an addition to staff. Each team receives a sheet of newsprint and marking pens in four colors. One team's *initial* brainstorming looks like the following:

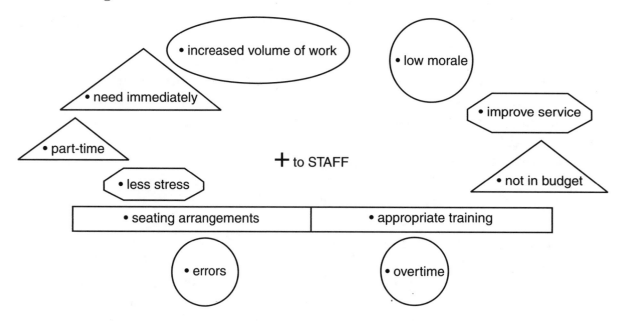

101 Ways to Make Training Active

Each team then groups similar topics using symbols: circles, triangles, squares, and octagons. The teams then organize the subtopics according to the proposal format:

△ Request: what, when, how much

- addition of part-time employee
- need immediately
- not in budget

◯ Rationale: why

- increased volume of work
- low morale—errors, overtime

▢ Implementation: how

- appropriate training
- seating arrangements

⬡ Benefits: to organization, manager, employees, customers

- improve service
- less stress

60 Action Learning

Procedure

1. Introduce the topic to the participants by providing some background information through a brief lecture and discussion.

2. Explain to the participants that you are going to give them an opportunity to experience the topic firsthand by making a "field trip" to a real-life setting relevant to the training.

3. Divide the group into subgroups of four or five and ask them to develop a list of questions and/or specific things they should look for during the field trip.

4. The subgroups put their questions or checklist items on flip-chart paper, post the paper, and share their ideas with the rest of the participants.

5. The group will then discuss the items and develop a common list for every person to use.

6. Give the participants a deadline (for example, one week) and direct them to visit a site, using the list of questions or checklist items to interview or observe. They may choose their own sites, or you may want to make specific assignments to avoid duplication or to get good distribution. For example, if the topic were customer service, participants could identify different types of organizations or businesses such as retail, fast food, restaurant, healthcare, hotel, car repair, and so on. They would

then visit these businesses as customers and, using their checklist, record their experiences.

7. Questions should be specific and lend themselves to comparison. Using the customer-service topic, the following questions would be appropriate:

   - How long did the employee take before acknowledging you (the customer)?
   - Did the employee smile?
   - Was the employee courteous and polite?
   - Did the employee ask open-ended questions to identify your needs?
   - Did the employee use active-listening techniques? Give examples.
   - Did the employee resolve any problems?
   - Were you as the customer pleased with the experience? Why or why not?

8. Ask the participants to share their findings with the rest of the group through some clever or creative method (for example, a skit, a mock interview, a panel discussion, or a game).

Variations

1. You may want to form teams of two or three participants instead of giving individual assignments.

2. Instead of the group's developing a common list of questions or observation guidelines, individuals could develop their own lists.

Case Example

In a training session on implementing the Americans with Disabilities Act (ADA), participants are given handouts and other information identifying architectural barriers to access and what business owners are required to do in order to make their buildings accessible.

The participants are divided into five subgroups with each subgroup assigned a particular "barrier": (1) entrances, (2) parking facilities, (3) work-spaces/lounges/lunchroom, (4) bathroom facilities, and (5) hallways.

Each subgroup develops its own checklist for the barrier assigned and identifies businesses to visit to ascertain if ADA guidelines are being met.

The subgroups developed the following checklists:

- Entrances

  _____ entrance ramp

  _____ doorknobs three feet from the ground

  _____ door light enough to be opened by someone in a wheelchair

- Parking Facilities

  _____ reserved parking spaces for people with disabilities

  _____ reserved parking spaces near the entrance to the building and twelve feet wide

  _____ curb cuts so that people in wheelchairs can pass easily

- Workspaces/Lounges/Lunchroom

  _____ aisles at least thirty-two inches wide

  _____ work stations, desks, tables, and so on high enough so that a person in a wheelchair can roll up close enough to sit comfortably

  _____ lunchroom and lounge accessible

- Bathroom Facilities

  _____ bathroom doorways at least thirty-three inches wide

  _____ sinks low enough to be used by someone in a wheelchair

  _____ grab bars in the bathroom stalls

- Hallways

  _____ fire alarms with flashing lights so that people with hearing impairments will know there is a fire

  _____ picture signs to show the purpose of each room so that people who cannot read will know where to go

  _____ braille markers on the doors and in the elevators

61 Learning Journals

Overview

When participants are asked to reflect in writing about the learning experiences they have undergone, they are encouraged to become conscious, through language, of what is happening to them. A widely used technique in this regard is a learning journal, a reflective log or diary participants keep over time.

Procedure

1. Explain to participants that experience is not necessarily "the best teacher" and that it is important for individuals to reflect on experiences to become conscious of what the experiences have taught them.

2. Invite the participants (or require them, if appropriate) to keep a journal of their reflections and learnings.

3. Suggest that participants write, twice a week, some of their thoughts and feelings about what they are learning. Tell them to record these comments as a personal diary (without worry about spelling, grammar, and punctuation).

4. Ask participants to focus on some or all of the following categories:

   - what's been **unclear** to them

   - what they **disagree** with

   - how the learning experiences **connect** with their personal lives

   - how the learning experiences are **reflected** in other things they read, see, or do

   - what they have **observed** about themselves or others since the learning experiences

   - what they **concluded** from the learning experiences

   - what they would like to **do** as a result of the learning experiences

5. Collect, read, and comment on the journals periodically so that participants are held accountable for keeping the journals and so that you can receive feedback about the participants' learnings.

Variations

1. Instead of a blank notebook, provide a structured form on which participants can organize their journal entries.

2. Ask participants to write during the session rather than outside the session.

Case Example

In a multi-session supervisory training program, the trainer thinks that the participants would benefit from keeping a learning journal throughout the program. The trainer identifies the topics that will be covered in the program and provides the participants with the following questions:

- What do you still need to know or understand about the topic?
- Based on the learnings in the program, what did you identify that you want to work on in dealing with those who report to you?
- Write a brief description of how you applied those learnings in your work environment.
- What worked? What didn't work?
- What changes did you notice in yourself?
- What changes did you experience in your relationships with your subordinates?
- What observations or conclusions do you have about the applicability of the training to your work situation?

The trainer suggests that each participant respond between sessions to some or all of the questions. The trainer collects the responses on an ongoing basis. At the end of the sessions, the trainer solicits input from the participants as to the value of keeping a journal.

62 Learning Contracts

+--+
| **Overview** |
| |
| Learning that is self-directed is often deeper |
| and more permanent than trainer-directed |
| learning. However, you should make sure that |
| the agreements about what and how something |
| will be learned are explicit. One means to |
| accomplish this is the learning contract. |
+--+

Procedure

1. Ask each participant to select a topic that he or she wants to study independently.

2. Encourage each participant to think through the plan of study carefully. Allow plenty of time for research and consultation in drawing up the plan.

3. Request that each participant submit a written contract that covers the following categories:

   ■ the learning objectives to be attained

   ■ the specific knowledge or skills to be mastered

   ■ the learning activities that will be utilized

   ■ the evidence that will be presented to show that the objectives have been achieved

   ■ a completion date

4. Meet with each participant and discuss the proposed contract. Suggest learning resources available to the participant. Negotiate any changes you would like to make.

Variations

1. Create group learning contracts instead of individual ones.

2. Instead of giving freedom of choice, select the topic and objectives for the participant or offer a limited selection. However, allow greater choice about how the topic will be studied.

Case Example

A trainer in a career-management program uses a learning contract to supplement the training of individual participants who are attending a multi-session outplacement workshop following organizational downsizing.

- Each participant identifies a specific area of career management that he or she wants to focus on and explore in more detail. Some of the choices include résumé writing, networking skills, interview skills, self-assessment, and career options.

- Although the workshop covers all of the above topics, each participant chooses the one area in which he or she wants additional help.

- The trainer provides books and other resources to help the participant plan and carry out the learning contract.

Below is a contract created by a participant who wants to work on his résumé.

SAMPLE CONTRACT:

Topic: Résumé Writing

Learning Objective: Present myself on paper in a favorable light

Specific Knowledge: Choose an appropriate format
Condense four pages into two
Write a clear career objective

Learning Activities: Review sample résumés
Choose those that I like and comment on them
Prepare a draft for critique by trainer
Rewrite as necessary
Send copies to three people and ask them to comment
Prepare final résumé

Completion Date: Within two weeks

AFFECTIVE LEARNING

Affective-learning activities help participants to examine their feelings, values, and attitudes. Even the most technical training topics involve affective learning. For example, what good is safety training without appreciating the importance of job safety? What good is computer training if participants are anxious and unsure of themselves? The strategies that follow are designed to raise awareness of the feelings, values, and attitudes that accompany many of today's training topics. These strategies gently push participants into examining their beliefs and asking themselves if they are committed to new ways of doing things.

63 Seeing How It Is

┌─ **Overview** ─────────────────┐

Often, a training program promotes understanding of
and sensitivity to people or situations that are unfamiliar
to participants. One of the best ways to accomplish this
goal is to create an affective activity that simulates that
unfamiliar person or situation.
└────────────────────────────────┘

Procedure

1. Choose a type of person or situation that you want participants to learn
   about. You may elect to have participants experience what it is like to be
   any of the following:

   - in the "minority"
   - in a different role or job function
   - from a different culture
   - a person with special problems or challenges

2. Create a way to simulate that person or situation. Among the ways to do
   this are the following:

   - Have participants dress in the attire of that person or situation. Or
     have them handle the equipment, props, accessories, or other belong-
     ings of that person or situation or engage in a typical activity.

   - Place participants in situations in which they are required to respond in
     the role or character they have been given.

   - Impersonate an individual and ask the participants to interview you and
     find out about your experiences, views, and feelings.

   - Use an analogy to build a simulation: Create a scenario that participants
     may be familiar with that sheds light on the unfamiliar situation. For
     example, you might ask all participants who are left-handed to portray
     people who are culturally different from the rest of the participants.

3. Ask participants how the simulation felt. Discuss the experience of being
   in someone else's shoes. Invite participants to identify the challenges
   that unfamiliar persons and situations present to them.

Variations

1. If possible, arrange for real encounters with the unfamiliar situation or person.

2. Conduct a mental-imagery experience in which participants visualize the person or situation with which they are unfamiliar.

Case Example

A simulation called "Instant Aging" is designed to sensitize participants to sensory deprivation and the normal process of aging. Participants are given eyeglasses smeared with Vaseline®, dried peas to put in their shoes, cotton for their ears, and latex gloves for their hands. Each participant is then asked to take out a pencil and paper and write down his or her name, address, telephone number, any medication currently being taken, and any known allergies. Next, the participants are told to take a walk outside the training room, opening the door and finding their way around. The simulation involves further directions concerning the specific details of the tasks participants are asked to perform and the manner in which they are to take turns assisting each other.

64 Billboard Ranking

Overview

Many learning situations contain no right or wrong answers. When values, opinions, ideas, and preferences exist about a topic you are teaching, this activity can be used to stimulate reflection and discussion.

Procedure

1. Divide participants into subgroups of four to six participants.

2. Give participants a numbered list of any of the following:

   - values (for example, 1. success, etc.)

   - opinions (for example, 1. "The federal deficit should be our major national concern," etc.)

   - actions to be taken in a specific situation (for example, "The steps to take in resuscitating someone who has stopped breathing are (1) give three or four rapid mouth-to-mouth artificial respirations," etc.)

   - solutions to a problem (for example, "Improve customer service in the hospital by (1) providing better signs so that customers can find their way around," etc.)

   - decision choices (for example, 1. cut the budget by 10 percent, etc.)

   - attributes (for example, 1. charismatic, etc.)

3. Give each subgroup a Post-it™ pad. Ask the subgroups to write the number of each item on the list on a separate sheet.

4. Next ask the subgroups to sort the sheets so that the number corresponding to the value, opinion, action, solution, decision, or attribute they most prefer is on top and the remaining items are placed consecutively in rank order.

5. Create a "billboard" on which subgroups can display their preferences. (The Post-it papers can be attached to a blackboard, a flip chart, or a large sheet of paper.)

6. Compare and contrast the rankings that are now visually displayed.

Variations

1. Attempt to achieve a full-group consensus.

2. Ask participants to interview members of subgroups whose rankings differ from theirs.

Case Example

A trainer for a session on hiring new employees presents the group with a list of goals a manager should consider when interviewing a candidate and asks the group to rank order the items according to their degree of importance:

1. to create a comfortable climate in which the candidate is able to speak freely

2. to give the candidate information about the job and the company

3. to get a clear picture of the candidate's ability to do the job based on past experience

4. to obtain behavioral information from the candidate

5. to determine if the candidate should be considered for the next step in the selection process

6. to identify personality characteristics and attitude factors as they relate to the job

After the billboard is created, the group then discusses the differences of opinion and how these varying areas of emphasis can influence the hiring decision.

65 **What? So What? Now What?**

Overview

The value of any experiential learning activity is enhanced by asking participants to reflect on the experience they just had and to explore its implications. This reflection period is often referred to as "processing" or "debriefing." Some experiential trainers now use the term "harvesting." Here is a three-stage sequence for harvesting a rich learning experience.

Procedure

1. Take the group through an experience that is appropriate to your topic. These experiences might include any of the following:

   - a game or simulation
   - a field trip
   - a video
   - an action-learning project
   - a debate
   - a role play
   - a mental-imagery activity

2. Ask participants to share **what** happened to them during the experience:

   - What did they do?
   - What did they observe? Think about?
   - What feelings did they have during the experience?

   Use any of the options listed in "Ten Methods for Obtaining Participation" (see page 16) to generate responses.

3. Next ask participants to ask themselves **"so what?"**

   - What benefits did they get from the experience?
   - What did they learn? Relearn?

- What are the implications of the activity?
- How does the experience (if it is a simulation or role play) relate to the real world?

 4. Finally, ask participants to consider **"now what?"**

- How do they want to do things differently in the future?
- How can they extend the learning?
- What steps can they take to apply what they learned?

Variations

1. Limit the discussion to **"what?"** and **"so what?"**

2. Use these questions to stimulate journal writing. (See strategy 61, "Learning Journals," page 197.)

Case Example

In a session on conflict resolution, participants are asked to form pairs. The trainer tells them that, at the sound of the whistle, the pairs are to engage in thumb wrestling for two minutes. At the end of the time period, the trainer blows the whistle again to stop the action. The trainer processes the activity by asking the following questions:

WHAT?

- How did you behave during the thumb wrestling?
- What feelings did you have as you were thumb wrestling?

SO WHAT?

- What did you learn about your own approach to conflict?
- How do you deal with conflict in real life?

NOW WHAT?

- How do you want to deal with conflict on the job or in your personal life in the future?

66 Active Self-Assessment

Overview

This activity provides an opportunity for the participants
to share their attitudes about a subject through self-
assessment. The activity allows the trainer to gauge
feelings and beliefs of the participants and serves as a
springboard for group discussion.

Procedure

1. Create a list of statements to be read to the participants that will assess
   their attitudes and feelings about a given subject. The following are
   some examples:

   - *I believe in "continuous process improvement."*

   - *Parents have the primary responsibility for their children's behavior.*

   - *I feel comfortable speaking in public.*

2. Ask the participants to stand in the back of the room, clearing away the
   chairs or desks to one side.

3. Create a rating scale of numbers one through five in the front of the
   room by using the blackboard or posting numbers on the wall.

4. Explain that statements will be read to the group and, after hearing each
   one, the participants should stand in front of the rating number that
   best matches their attitude about or knowledge of the subject. Depending on the subject matter, number "1" could be "Strongly Agree" or
   "Fully Understand," with the range extending to "5" for "Strongly
   Disagree" or "Do Not Understand."

5. As each statement is read, participants should move to stand near the
   number that best matches their knowledge or opinion. After lines form
   in front of the various positions, invite some participants to share why
   they have chosen that position.

6. After hearing the opinions of others, invite anyone who wishes to alter
   his or her position on the scale to do so.

7. Continue reading the individual statements or facts, requesting that participants move to the number that best matches their opinion or knowledge.

8. When you have finished reading all of the statements, break participants into subgroups. Give them a written copy of the statements to discuss.

9. Now ask participants to privately reconsider their choices on each item. Have them assign a number to each statement that reflects their final level of agreement or disagreement.

Variations

1. In a larger setting, have the participants first choose a response privately to the statements and then move to the numbered posts to reveal their positions.

2. Begin with small-group discussion and then proceed with individual (private) assessment.

Case Example

During a career development workshop, participants are asked to assess their career values three times: (1) publicly, (2) in small groups, and (3) in private.
The group uses the following scale:

> 1 = Strongly Agree
> 2 = Agree
> 3 = Neither Agree nor Disagree
> 4 = Disagree
> 5 = Strongly Disagree

The trainer reads the following statements:

- I want a job that allows me to work with other people.
- I want a job that pays me the most I can get given my skills.
- I want a job that is secure and free from worry about constant evaluation.
- I want a job that I do not have to take home at night.
- I want a job that does not involve a lot of commuting and travel.
- I want a job that has value to the community.
- I want a job that constantly challenges my abilities.

67 Role Models

┌─────────────────────── **Overview** ───────────────────────┐

This activity is an interesting way to stimulate discussion about values and attitudes. Participants are asked to nominate well-known personalities as role models of traits associated with the training topic.

└──┘

Procedure

1. Divide participants into subgroups of five or six and give each subgroup a sheet of newsprint and markers.

2. Ask each subgroup to identify three people as being representative of the subject under discussion. Examples are well-known leaders, creative people, management gurus, and so on.

3. After the subgroups have identified three well-known figures, ask them to make a list of the characteristics the three have in common that qualify them as examples or role models. The subgroups are to post their lists of people and characteristics.

4. Reconvene the entire group and compare lists, asking each subgroup to explain why it chose the people it did.

5. Lead the entire group in a discussion of the varied perceptions among the participants.

Variations

1. Instead of citing real people, ask the subgroups to choose fictional characters.

2. Assign each subgroup a specific list of people who are representative of the subject under discussion.

Case Example

In a session on leadership, the trainer begins by asking managers to indicate, by a show of hands, if they would rather be known as "good managers" or "good leaders."

The trainer then conducts a brief full-group discussion on what the managers perceive to be the difference between a manager and a leader.

Without defining leadership at this point, the trainer breaks the group into subgroups and asks each subgroup to identify three people (real or fictional) that they would label "leaders" and then to identify common characteristics among the three.

After comparing the subgroup lists, the trainer helps the entire group establish a composite list of characteristics of effective leaders.

Skill Development

The bottom line in most training programs is the acquisition of skills. When participants are struggling to learn new skills, whether technical or nontechnical, they need to practice them effectively and to obtain useful performance feedback. The strategies that follow represent different ways to develop skills. Some are intense and some are fun. In particular, different role-playing designs are featured.

68 The Firing Line

Overview

This is a lively, fast-moving format that can be used for a variety of purposes, such as testing or role playing. It features continually rotating pairs. Participants get the opportunity to respond to rapidly fired questions or other types of challenges.

Procedure

1. Decide on the purpose for which you would like to use "the firing line." For example, if your goal is skill development, you can have the participants use this activity to do any of the following:

   - to test or drill one another
   - to role play a situation assigned to them
   - to teach one another

   You can also have participants use this strategy for other purposes:

   - to interview others to obtain their views and opinions
   - to discuss a short text or quotation

2. Arrange chairs in two facing rows. Have enough chairs for all the participants.

3. Separate the chairs into clusters of three to five on each side or row. The arrangement might look like the following:

4. Distribute to each "x" participant a card containing a task or assignment that he or she will instruct the "y" person opposite him or her to respond to. Use one of the following:

- a test question (for example, ask the person opposite you to tell you the correct safety procedure for fire evacuation)

- a character to role play (for example, ask the person opposite you to portray a supervisor telling a subordinate to redo a report)

- a teaching assignment (for example, ask the person opposite you to teach you the Heimlich maneuver)

- an interview topic (for example, ask the person opposite you this question: "How do you feel about the changes we've recently made in our ordering process?")

- a short text or quotation (for example, ask the person opposite you his or her opinion about the statement "The customer is always right.")

You should give a different card to each "x" member of a cluster. For example, there will be four different role-playing situations in a cluster of four.

5. Begin the first assignment. After a brief period of time, announce that it is time for all the "y's" to rotate one chair to the left (or right) within the cluster. Do not rotate the "x's." Have the "x" person "fire" his or her assignment or task to the "y" person opposite him or her. Continue for as many rounds as you have different tasks.

Variations

1. Reverse roles so that the "x" participants become the "y" participants and vice versa.

2. In some situations, it may be interesting and appropriate to give the same assignment to each cluster member. In this instance, the "y" participant will be asked to respond to the same instructions as each member of his or her cluster. For example, a participant could be asked to role play the same situation a number of times.

Case Example

In a presentation skills session, the instructor is training participants to maintain good eye contact and to speak fluently. The instructor gives to the "x" members of each cluster one of the following cards:

- Ask the person opposite you to give his or her views about the country's current president.

- Ask the person opposite you to tell you about his or her childhood.

- Ask the person opposite you to explain the features and benefits of the toothpaste he or she uses.

- Ask the person opposite you to tell you about his or her hobbies and interests.

69 Active Observation and Feedback

Overview

The usual procedure when utilizing observers in role-playing activities or skill-practice sessions is to wait until the performance is over before inviting feedback. Instead, the procedure in this activity gives performers immediate feedback. It also keeps observers on their toes during the performance.

Procedure

1. Develop a role-playing activity in which some participants practice a skill while others observe.

2. Provide the observers with a checklist of positive and negative behaviors to watch for. Instruct the observers to give a signal to the role players when a desired behavior occurs and a different signal when an undesired behavior takes place. Some examples of signals that can be used are the following:

   - raising hands
   - whistling
   - snapping fingers
   - clapping

3. Explain that the purpose of the signals is to provide *immediate feedback* to the role players concerning their performance.

4. After the role play is finished, discuss the experience with the role players. Find out if the immediate feedback helped or hindered them.

Variations

1. Allow observers to use a signal (for example, blowing a whistle) to freeze the action of the role play and to ask questions or give more detailed feedback to the role players.

2. Videotape the role plays. Do not permit any active forms of feedback during the taping. Have participants watch the tapes and use the established signals during the replay.

Case Example

In a selling skills session, the trainer gives to observers the following checklist of positive and negative behaviors:

- Desired behaviors
  - using customer's name
  - maintaining eye contact
  - asking open-ended questions
  - clarifying and confirming
  - smiling
  - pacing and mirroring the customer's style

- Undesired behaviors
  - trying to sell too early
  - speaking too fast
  - using jargon
  - using distracting gestures and mannerisms
  - using verbal pauses ("ums" and "uhs")

The signal for a desired behavior is a bell; for an undesired behavior, a kazoo.

When the observers signal, the action stops and the observers hold up a card with a number from 1 to 4 indicating an instant rating (4 = highest; 1 = lowest).

70 Nonthreatening Role Playing

> **┌─── Overview ───┐**
>
> This technique reduces the threat of role playing by placing the trainer in the lead role and involving the group in providing the responses and setting the scenario's direction.

Procedure

1. Create a role play in which you will demonstrate desired behaviors for a task, such as handling an irate customer complaining to a customer-service representative.

2. Inform the group that you will do the role play. The participants' job is to help you deal with the situation.

3. Start the role play but stop at frequent intervals and ask the group to give you feedback and direction. Do not hesitate to ask participants to provide specific "lines" for you to utilize. For example, at a specific point, say "What should I say next?" Listen to the suggestions and try one of them out.

4. Continue the role play so that participants increasingly coach you in handling the situation. This gives them skill practice while you do the actual role playing for them.

Variations

1. Using the same procedure, have the group coach a fellow participant (instead of the trainer).

2. Videotape the entire role play. Play it back and discuss with participants other ways to respond at specific points in the situation.

Case Example

Social workers are learning how to conduct an intake interview with first-time clients. The trainer assumes the role of the social worker, with a group member playing the client. After the initial interaction between the social worker and the client, the role play is stopped and group members are asked by the trainer to suggest additional questions for the social worker to ask the client, such as "What services do you think you most need?" or "When did this problem first occur?"

The role play continues and is stopped intermittently for the group to provide additional questions for the social worker to ask. The trainer discusses with the group potential responses to their questions. The group also provides feedback on the style of interaction, such as "The client seems very intimidated by the social worker. Try to make him feel more comfortable."

71 Triple Role Playing

┌─────────────────── **Overview** ───────────────────┐

This technique expands traditional role playing by utilizing three different participants in the same role play. It
shows the effect of individual style variation on a situation's outcome.

└──┘

Procedure

1. With the assistance of a willing participant, demonstrate the basic technique of role playing (if needed) with a situation such as an employee
   protesting a performance review with his or her supervisor.

2. Create the scenario and describe it to the participants.

3. Ask for four participants to assume the character roles in the role play.
   Assign one person to be the primary character (the supervisor) and instruct the remaining three individuals that they will all play the remaining role (the employee) on a rotating basis.

4. Ask the three rotating participants to leave the room and decide the
   order in which they will engage in the role play. When ready, the first
   participant reenters the room and begins the role play.

5. After three minutes, call time and ask for the second rotating participant
   to enter the room and repeat the same situation. The first participant
   may now remain in the room. After three minutes with the second participant, continue with the third participant repeating the scenario.

6. At the conclusion, ask the group to compare and contrast the styles of
   the three employee role players by identifying which techniques were
   effective and noting areas for improvement.

Variations

1. Instead of holding a full-group discussion, divide the participants into
   three subgroups. Assign one of the three rotating role players to each

subgroup. Ask the members of each subgroup to give the person assigned to them supportive feedback. Use this procedure when you want to reduce the potential embarrassment of publicly comparing the role players.

2. For a larger group, divide the participants into three sections and follow the rotation of triple role playing, with the volunteers rotating among the three groups. Assign one member of each section to play the role of supervisor. The group can then reconvene to compare and contrast the three styles.

Case Example

In a session on managing diversity, the trainer is helping participants learn how to confront offensive behavior in the workplace.

- The trainer sets the scene by describing the following situation:

   You are at lunch with George Smith, a colleague from another department. He relates the following:

   I'll sure hate to lose my secretary. She's such a bright, capable girl. She hasn't said anything yet, but I know her husband just finished school, so she'll probably quit. I'll have her a few months or maybe a year and then she'll quit to stay home and have a baby. It's too bad. She likes her job and she makes good money for a woman.

- The trainer asks for someone to play the role of George Smith and for three volunteers to play the other manager.

- The three volunteers leave the room and decide among themselves the order in which they will role play the situation.

- The first volunteer enters the room and responds to the person playing George Smith.

- The same scenario is repeated two more times, with the same amount of time allowed for each role play.

- At the end of the last role play, the trainer leads a discussion comparing the three different styles displayed. The group notes which techniques were the most appropriate and effective in dealing with offensive behavior.

72 Rotating Roles

Overview

This activity is an excellent way of giving each participant an opportunity to practice skills through role playing real-life situations.

Procedure

1. Divide the participants into subgroups of three and position them throughout the room with as much space between subgroups as possible.

2. Ask each trio to create three real-life scenarios dealing with the topic you have been discussing. Stipulate that each scenario contain a primary and a secondary role. The third member of each trio will act as observer.

3. After each trio has written its three scenarios on three separate sheets of paper, one member from each trio delivers the scenarios to the next trio and is available to clarify or provide additional information if necessary. The participant then returns to his or her original trio.

4. On a rotating basis, each member of the trios will have an opportunity to practice a different role in the three different scenarios.

5. Each round should consist of at least ten minutes of role playing with five to ten minutes of feedback from the observer. Determine the length of each round based on time constraints, the topic, and the skill level of the participants.

6. In each round, the observer should concentrate on identifying what the primary player did well in using the concepts and skills learned in the session and what he or she can do to improve.

7. After all three rounds have been completed, reconvene the entire group for a general discussion of the key learning points and the value of the activity.

Variations

1. You can prepare scenarios instead of having each subgroup write them.

2. Prepare an observer feedback sheet identifying specific skills and techniques that the observer should look for.

Case Example

Participants in a communication skills session are asked to break into trios and develop three work-related scenarios in which people are required to practice active-listening skills.

- The following are some general situations on which the trios build their scenarios:
  - receiving directions on how to get from one place to another
  - receiving negative feedback about a performance problem
  - receiving instructions on how to do something
  - receiving information about a new policy or procedure
  - receiving a complaint from an employee about a coworker
- The trios determine specifics as to who the communicators are, where they are, what their states of mind are, and why this conversation is taking place.
- The scenarios are exchanged among trios and practiced. In each round of role playing, the observer concentrates on how well the listener uses active-listening techniques such as confirming and clarifying with statements like "What I hear you saying...," "As I understand it...," "Let me make sure I understand what you are saying...," and so forth.
- In debriefing, the observer points out specific examples of when the listener used these techniques and offers suggestions of when it would have been appropriate to use the techniques.

73 Modeling the Way

```
┌─────────────────────── Overview ───────────────────────┐
│                                                         │
│  This technique gives participants an opportunity to prac-│
│  tice, through demonstration, specific skills taught in the│
│  course. Demonstration is often an appropriate alterna-  │
│  tive to role playing because it is less threatening. Partici-│
│  pants are given ample time to create their own scenarios│
│  and determine how they want to illustrate specific skills│
│  and techniques.                                         │
│                                                         │
└─────────────────────────────────────────────────────────┘
```

Procedure

1. Following learning activities on a given topic, identify several general situations where the participants might be required to use the skills just discussed.

2. Divide the participants into subgroups according to the number of people necessary to demonstrate a given scenario. In most cases, two or three people will be required.

3. Give the subgroups ten to fifteen minutes to create their scenarios.

4. The subgroups will also determine how they are going to demonstrate the skill to the group. Give them five to seven minutes to practice.

5. Each subgroup will take turns delivering its demonstration to the rest of the group. Allow the opportunity for feedback after each demonstration.

Variations

1. You can create subgroups of more people than are necessary for the demonstration, with those not performing serving as creators of the scenarios, directors, and advisers.

2. You can create the scenarios and assign them to specific subgroups.

Case Example

In an assertiveness training course, a trainer identifies the following general situations in which a person might want to be assertive as well as the number of people necessary to demonstrate the skill:

- saying "no" (two people)
- breaking into a conversation (three or four people)
- preventing someone from interrupting (three or four people)
- giving negative feedback (two people)
- disagreeing (two or three people)
- receiving criticism (two people)

Subgroups are given seven to ten minutes to create their own specific scenarios and to decide how they are going to demonstrate being assertive in the particular situation.

Members from each subgroup take a turn demonstrating their ability to be assertive to the rest of the group.

At the completion of each demonstration, the entire group comments on what the subgroup did well and offers suggestions for improvement.

74 Silent Demonstration

Overview

This strategy is particularly useful when you are doing any kind of procedural training. By demonstrating a procedure as silently as possible, you encourage participants to be mentally alert.

Procedure

1. Decide on a multi-step procedure you want participants to learn. You might choose any of the following:

   - using a computer application

   - filling out an office requisition form

   - operating machinery

   - taking applications from customers

   - performing any work-related action that involves physical effort

2. Ask the participants to watch you perform the entire procedure. Just do it, with little or no explanation or commentary about what and why you are doing what you do. (Telling the participants what you are doing will lessen their mental alertness.) Give the participants a visual glimpse of the "big picture" or the entire job. Do not expect retention. At this point, you are merely establishing readiness for learning.

3. Form the participants into pairs. Demonstrate the first part of the procedure again, with little or no explanation or commentary. *Ask pairs to discuss with each other what they observed you doing.* Obtain a volunteer to explain what you did. If the participants have difficulty following the procedure, demonstrate again. Acknowledge correct observations.

4. Have the pairs practice with each other the first part of the procedure. When it is mastered, proceed with a silent demonstration of the remaining parts of the procedure, following each part with paired practice.

Variations

1. If possible, ask participants to attempt the procedure before any demonstration. Encourage guesses and an openness to making mistakes. By doing this, you will immediately get participants mentally involved. Then have them watch you demonstrate.

2. If some participants master the procedure sooner than others, recruit them as "silent demonstrators."

Case Example

The trainer in a bank-teller training session demonstrates how to enter new account information into the on-line system. In addition to customer information such as name, address, social security number, and telephone number, other coded information (account type, other related accounts or services, lockouts or restrictions) is also entered with no explanation given.

Pairs discuss with each other what they observed and speculate on what the various codes mean and why the information is important. One example is an account in the name of a child. A parent's signature is required for a withdrawal. The account must be coded in the system to prevent access by the child without a parent's permission. This is protection for both the account owner and the bank.

75 Practice-Rehearsal Pairs

Overview

This is a simple strategy for practicing and rehearsing any skill or procedure with a learning partner. The goal is to ensure that both partners can perform the skill or procedure.

Procedure

1. Select a set of skills or procedures you want participants to master. Form the participants into pairs. Within each pair, assign two roles: (1) explainer or demonstrator and (2) checker.

2. The explainer or demonstrator explains and/or demonstrates how to perform any specified skill or procedure. The checker verifies that the explanation and/or demonstration is correct, encourages his or her partner, and provides coaching, if needed.

3. The partners reverse roles. The new explainer/demonstrator is given another skill or procedure to perform.

4. The process continues until all the skills are rehearsed.

Variations

1. Use a multi-step skill or procedure instead of a set of several distinct ones. Have one partner perform the first step and have the other partner perform the next step until the sequence of steps is completed.

2. When the pairs have completed their work, arrange a demonstration before the group.

This technique is based on "Drill-Review Pairs" by David W. Johnson, Roger T. Johnson, and Karl A. Smith.

Case Example

In a course on communication, the instructor has demonstrated effective and ineffective words to use when attempting to persuade others. Participants are divided into pairs. The demonstrator's job is to show his or her partner how to discuss the status of a project that has been assigned to an employee. The checker's job is to use the following chart to verify that the demonstration "offers options" rather than "cuts off options." The pair then reverses roles and repeats the exercise.

Offers Options	Cuts Off Options
Will you...?	You have to....
I am unable to because....	You can't....
However....	It's not our policy....
What have you considered?	Why don't you...?
It works well when....	You're required....

76 I Am the _____

```
┌─────────────────── Overview ───────────────────┐
│                                                 │
│  In this strategy, participants assume the      │
│  role of a person whose job they are learning   │
│  about. Participants are given realistic        │
│  on-the-job assignments with little prior       │
│  instruction and learn "by doing."              │
│                                                 │
└─────────────────────────────────────────────────┘
```

Procedure

1. Choose the role you want participants to perform. The following are some examples:

   I am the   *bank teller*
   claims adjuster
   performance reviewer
   service representative
   team leader
   receptionist
   sales manager
   warehouse supervisor
   benefits coordinator

2. Prepare written instructions explaining one or several tasks that might be assigned to that role. For example, a bank teller might be asked to "split a deposit."

3. Pair up participants and distribute the assignments to each pair. Set a time limit for the activity. Provide reference materials to help the participants complete the assignments.

4. Reconvene the full group and discuss the assignments.

Variations

1. Allow participants to leave the room and obtain coaching from fellow employees who can serve as resources.

101 Ways to Make Training Active

2. Have participants do the tasks alone, without the support of a partner.

Case Example

In a train-the-trainer program, participants are paired up and given the following assignment. An extensive training library is available to them.

You are being considered for a position as a course designer for a well-known company. The company is seeking people who are versatile and creative. Above all else, it wants designers whose designs "deliver" on the objectives promised. To assess your design skills, the company has given you the following task:

Put together a twenty-minute design that achieves each of the following four objectives. Assume that the design occurs during the middle of a longer training sequence and that requisite knowledge for the design has already been accomplished. **Keep your design limited to the objectives specified.**

1. Participants are to **obtain feedback** from others about their nonverbal communication.

2. Participants will **get in touch with their feelings** about confronting other adults (for example, problem employees).

3. Participants will **be informed** about techniques for increasing the effectiveness of a meeting.

4. Participants will **practice skills** for facilitating discussions.

77 Curveballs

Overview

This is a dramatic way to practice skills associated with one's job. It places participants in difficult situations that they must figure out how to escape or resolve.

Procedure

1. Select a situation that is common to the job performed by participants. Examples include the following:

   - leading a meeting
   - giving an assignment to an employee
   - getting an assignment from a manager
   - making a presentation
   - giving a report to a manager
   - talking to a customer

2. Recruit a volunteer to role play a specific situation. Be sure to explain the situation in detail.

3. Hand out instructions to other participants that direct them to "throw curveballs" at the volunteer. Specify some actions that can be taken to give the volunteer a difficult time handling the situation. Do not let the volunteer see the "curveball" instructions.

4. Allow the volunteer to cope with the situation. Applaud his or her efforts. Discuss with the entire group ways to deal with the unanticipated events.

5. Recruit new volunteers and present different challenges to them.

Variations

1. Invite the participants to select their own "curveballs" to throw at the volunteers.

2. Instead of using volunteers, demonstrate yourself how to handle the "curveballs" thrown by participants.

Case Example

In a session on facilitation skills for team leaders, the trainer asks for a volunteer participant to lead a meeting during which team members are to establish group norms or codes of conduct for their team meetings. The volunteer facilitator is asked to step out of the room while the rest of the group decides on one person to act the part of a negative or hostile participant and another to try to engage the person next to him or her in a side conversation. The volunteer facilitator then comes back into the room and is challenged to cope with these two difficult people while leading the meeting.

78 Advisory Group

Overview

This is a strategy for obtaining ongoing feedback during a skill-based training program. All too often, trainers solicit participant feedback after the training has been completed—too late to make any adjustments.

Procedure

1. Establish times when you would like to obtain feedback, such as during breaks, at lunchtime, or after a day session of a multi-day program.

2. Ask for a small group of volunteers to meet with you. Tell them their job is to solicit the reactions of other participants before the meeting time.

3. Direct the volunteers to use questions such as the following:

   - What skills have been helpful? Unhelpful?
   - Which skills need more explanation?
   - What would help you to learn the skills better?
   - Are you ready to move on to new skills?
   - Are the skills sufficiently related to your job?
   - What would you like more of tomorrow?
   - What would you like less of?
   - What would you like to continue?

Variations

1. Try out a skill-practice activity or demonstration with the "advisory group" that you are planning to use for the entire group. Obtain reactions.

2. Use other alternatives for obtaining ongoing feedback, such as postmeeting reaction surveys or an oral survey of participant reactions.

Case Example

In a multi-session process-improvement program, participants all take turns serving on an advisory group that meets with the trainer to discuss what has gone well and what areas still need to be clarified or refined. In one such meeting, the members of the advisory group express confusion about the roles and responsibilities of the following people: process sponsor, process owner, facilitator, and team members.

The advisory group members indicate that before they move on to the actual steps in process improvement, they need to have these roles defined and clarified by relating them to familiar roles in a traditional structure. The trainer explains that the *process sponsor* is the person who identifies the process that needs to be improved; the *process owner* has the final "ownership" or accountability for the process; the *facilitator* is someone outside the group who is responsible for coaching the group and helping them approach the process improvement according to the prescribed steps; *team members* are representatives from various departments that are affected by the process to be improved. These team members form a cross-functional team.

How to Make Training Unforgettable

REVIEWING STRATEGIES

One of the surest ways to make training "stick" is to allow time for participants to review material that has been learned. In fact, material that has been reviewed by participants is five times as likely to be retained as material that has not. Reviewing allows participants to "save" the information in their brains. What follows is an array of strategies that promote review. In addition to being active, these strategies all make reviewing fun.

79 Index Card Match

Overview

This is an active, enjoyable way to review course material. It allows participants to pair up and quiz the rest of the group.

Procedure

1. Write down on separate index cards the names of techniques and/or concepts examined in the training session (for example, "fishbowl discussion" and "reengineering"). Create enough cards to equal one-half the number of participants.

2. On separate cards, write clear definitions of each of the techniques or concepts you have chosen **or** give a clear example of the technique or concept. For example, a fishbowl discussion is "a way to have a small-group discussion in a large-group setting."

3. Combine the two sets of cards and shuffle them several times so that they are well mixed.

4. Give out one card to each participant. Explain that this is a matching activity. Some participants have the names of techniques or concepts examined in the training session and others have definitions or examples.

5. Direct participants to find their matching cards. When a match is formed, ask each pair of participants to find seats together. (Tell them not to reveal to other participants what is contained on their cards.)

6. When all the matching pairs have been seated, have pair members quiz the rest of the group on their technique or concept by reading aloud its definition or example.

Variations

1. Develop cards containing a sentence with a missing word to be matched to cards containing the missing word. For example, one card might say

"Many salespeople fail to _____ after a sale" and its matching card would say "follow up."

2. Develop cards containing questions with several possible answers. For example, one question might be "What are ways to defuse a conflict?" Match each card to a corresponding card that contains an assortment of answers. When pair members quiz the group, have them obtain several answers from the participants.

Case Example

In a session on total quality management, the trainer develops the following list of analytical tools and their definitions:

- **Affinity Diagram**—Organizes ideas into natural groupings; categories and new ideas are generated by team members working silently.

- **Cause-and-Effect Diagram**—Used to identify root causes of the effect being analyzed.

- **Pareto Diagram**—Organizes causes by frequency; also known as 80/20 rule.

- **Histogram**—Shows frequency of occurrence of different measurements for a given quality attribute; used to depict variation in an observed measurement.

- **Scatter Diagram**—Depicts the relationship between variables, thereby helping to substantiate whether root cause is related to effect.

- **Control Diagram**—Used to determine whether or not variation is due to common or special causes.

- **Flow Diagram**—Used to understand a process by depicting its various activities and decision points.

- **Relations Diagram**—Display of the cause-and-effect relationship between factors in a complex situation.

- **Tree Diagram**—Displays range of subtasks needed to achieve objective.

To create an index-card matching activity, the trainer writes each tool on a card and the definition on a separate card. The cards are combined and shuffled. Each participant receives a card (either a term or a definition) and then finds its match.

80 Flip Chart/Overhead Review

Overview

This strategy challenges participants to comment on the flip chart/overhead content you have used during a training session. It is an excellent way to help participants revisit the content you have covered.

Procedure

1. At the end of a training session, flip back to the beginning of your flip chart or display the first of your transparencies.

2. Ask participants to recall what the flip-chart sheet or transparency is about. Ask questions such as the following:

   ■ What does this refer to? (*Note:* This is especially fun when a sheet or transparency is scribbled.)

   ■ Why is it important?

   ■ Who can give me an example of this?

   ■ What value does this have for you?

3. Continue until you have reviewed all the course material (or as much as there is time and audience interest for).

4. As you proceed through the content, make any final remarks.

Variations

1. Have partners or subgroups discuss each sheet or transparency instead of using a full-group process.

2. If there are ten or fewer participants, invite them to gather around the flip chart or overhead projector and conduct their own review of the material. To give them the sense that the review is not a test, consider leaving the room while the process is going on. This will empower the participants to use the time as they see fit.

Case Example

Near the end of a session on decision making, the trainer asks participants to review and react to four transparencies that were shown during the training program:

Types of Decisions ■ routine ■ crisis ■ analytical ■ creative ■ negotiated ■ arbitrary	**Reasons People Find Decision Making Difficult** ■ lack of confidence ■ fear of being disliked ■ fear of retaliation
Who Makes Decisions ■ one person ■ more than one person ■ a group	**Factors Influencing Decision Making** ■ personal values ■ risk tolerance ■ past experience ■ political climate ■ constraints—time, money, etc.

81 Giving Questions and Getting Answers

Overview

This is a team-building strategy to involve participants in the review of learning material from a previous session or at the end of a workshop.

Procedure

1. Hand out two index cards to each participant.

2. Ask each participant to complete the following sentences:

   Card 1: I still have a question about _____.

   Card 2: I can answer a question about _____.

3. Create subgroups and have each subgroup select the most pertinent question and the most interesting answer from the cards of its members.

4. Ask each subgroup to report the question it has selected. Determine if anyone in the full group can answer the question. If not, the trainer should respond.

5. Ask each subgroup to report the answer it has selected. Have the subgroup members share it with the rest of the group.

Variations

1. Prepare, in advance, several "question cards" and distribute them to the subgroups. Ask subgroup members to choose one or more questions that they are capable of answering.

2. Prepare, in advance, several "answer cards" and distribute them to the subgroups. Ask subgroup members to choose one or more answers that they find helpful in reviewing what they have learned.

Case Example

Subgroups in a session on coping with change select the following questions and answers:

Questions

I still have a question about...

- how to cope with my fears about all the new technology involved with my job.
- what I can do to reduce the stress of adjusting to a new manager.
- how to determine what can be controlled or influenced and what cannot.

Answers

I can answer a question about...

- the difference between limiting beliefs and empowering beliefs.
- why people resist change.
- how to use change to your advantage.

82 Crossword Puzzle

Overview

Designing a review test as a crossword puzzle invites immediate engagement and participation. A crossword puzzle
can be completed individually or in teams.

Procedure

1. Brainstorm several key terms or names related to the training session
   you have completed.

2. Construct a simple crossword puzzle, including as many of these items as
   you can. Darken spaces you do not need. (*Note:* If it is too difficult to create a crossword puzzle with these items, include items not related to the
   training session as fillers.)

3. Create clues for your crossword items. Use any of the following kinds of
   clues:

   - a short definition ("a test used to establish reliability")
   - a category in which the item fits ("a kind of fixed asset")
   - an example ("a Gantt chart is an example of this")
   - an opposite ("the opposite of groupthink")

4. Distribute the puzzle to participants and ask them to complete it, either
   individually or in teams.

5. Set a time limit. Award a prize to the individual or team that has the
   most correct items.

Variations

1. Have the entire group work cooperatively to complete the crossword
   puzzle.

2. Simplify the puzzle by deciding on one word that has been key to the
   entire training session. Write it in horizontal crossword squares. Choose

words that summarize other points in the training session and fit them vertically through the key word.

Case Example

In a training session for customer-service representatives at a bank, the trainer creates a crossword puzzle to review the information presented. He uses the following clues:

ACROSS

1. If you don't have money to buy services, you have to _____ + ing

3. Another word for cash

5. A type of loan used for one-time borrowing needs

6. No collateral pledged

8. An installment loan is a _____ end loan

11. Another word for money owed

DOWN

1. The date the loan will be paid in full

2. A loan that has collateral

4. _____worthy

7. Home_____ loan

9. A type of collateral

10. Releasing a lien on the books in a court house

83 Jeopardy Review

Overview

This strategy is designed like the popular television game show—answers are given and the challenge is to come up with the correct questions. The format can easily be used as a review of course material.

Procedure

1. Create three to six categories of review questions. Use any of the following generic categories:

   - Concepts or Ideas

   - Facts

   - Skills

   - Names

   Or create categories by topic. For example, a course on meeting management might involve topics such as "Before Meetings," "During Meetings," and "After Meetings."

2. Develop at least three answers (and their corresponding questions) per category. For example, the answer "This should always be circulated before meetings" can be matched to the question "What is an agenda?" You don't need to have the same number of questions and answers in each category. However, you should develop questions and answers of increasing difficulty.

3. Show a Jeopardy game board on an overhead transparency or flip chart. Announce the categories and the point values for each answer. The following is a sample game board:

This technique was created by Rebecca Birch and Cynthia Denton-Ade.

Before Meetings	During Meetings	After Meetings
10 points	10 points	10 points
20 points	20 points	20 points
30 points	30 points	30 points

4. Form teams of three to six participants and provide a responder card for each team. If possible, create teams comprised of individuals that represent a range of skill levels, experience, and functional areas in the organization.

5. Ask each team to choose a team captain and a team scorekeeper.

   ■ *Team captains* represent the team. They are the only ones who can hold up the responder card and give an answer. **Team captains must confer with team members before giving an answer.**

   ■ *Scorekeepers* are responsible for adding and subtracting points for their team.

   Note: As the game moderator, you are responsible for keeping track of which questions have been asked. As each question is used, cross it off the game board. Put a check mark next to any questions participants have difficulty answering. You can come back to these questions when the game is over.

6. Review the following rules of the game:

   ■ The team captain who holds up the responder card first gets the opportunity to answer.

   ■ All answers must be given in the form of a question.

   ■ If the correct response is given, the point value for that category is awarded. If the response is incorrect, the point value is deducted from the team's score, and the other teams have an opportunity to answer.

   ■ The team that gives the last correct response controls the board.

101 Ways to Make Training Active

Variations

1. Instead of using team captains, have each member of the team take a turn playing the game. He or she cannot consult with team members before answering.

2. Have participants create the game questions.

Case Example

In a business writing course the instructor creates the following three categories with answers and questions:

Letters and Memos

1. This letter format has four parts in the body.
   - What is a "bad news" letter?

2. This closing is preferred in business letters.
   - What is "sincerely"?

Grammar

1. A grammatical construction in which the subject is doing the action.
   - What is active voice?

2. This type of sentence is constructed by two independent clauses joined by "and," "but," or "or."
   - What is a compound sentence?

Punctuation

1. This punctuation mark should always follow the salutation in a business letter.
   - What is a colon?

2. This punctuation mark can take the place of a conjunction in a compound sentence.
   - What is a semicolon?

84 College Bowl

Overview

This strategy is a twist on the standard review of material. It allows the trainer to evaluate the extent to which participants have mastered the material and serves to reinforce, clarify, and summarize key points.

Procedure

1. Divide the participants into teams of three or four members and have each team select a college (or sports team, company, car, etc.) to represent.

2. Provide each participant with an index card. Participants will hold up their cards to indicate that they want a chance to answer a question. The format of the game is known as a "toss up." This means that every time you ask a question, any member of any team can indicate his or her desire to answer.

3. Explain the following rules:
   - To answer a question, raise your card.
   - You can raise your card before a question has been fully stated if you think you know the answer. As soon as you interrupt, the reading of the question is stopped.
   - Teams score one point for each member's correct response.
   - When someone answers incorrectly, another team gets to answer. (The team can hear the entire question if the previous team has interrupted the reading.)

4. After all of the questions have been asked, tally the scores and announce a winner.

This technique was created by Rebecca Birch and Cynthia Denton-Ade.

101 Ways to Make Training Active

5. Based on the responses from the game, review any material that is unclear or that needs reinforcement.

Variations

1. Ask questions of each team in turn instead of using a "toss up" format.

2. Use the game to test whether participants can perform a skill correctly rather than answer a cognitive question.

Case Example ─────────────────────────────────

In a session on performance management, participants are formed into three teams for a "College Bowl" review. The teams decide to call themselves *Tigers, Panthers,* and *Bulldogs.* The trainer uses the following questions in a "toss up" format:

1. How much time should a performance-appraisal interview take?

2. In documenting an employee's performance, what type of file should the manager keep?

3. What is one of the ABCs of documentation?

4. Where should an appraisal interview be conducted?

5. What percentage of the time should a manager talk during a performance-appraisal interview?

6. Who should determine the performance-improvement plan?

7. Who is responsible for the growth and development of the employee?

8. When should a manager give an employee feedback about his or her performance?

85 Participant Recap

Overview

This strategy gives participants the opportunity to summarize what they have learned and to present their summaries to others. It is a good way to get participants to recap the training on their own.

Procedure

1. Explain to participants that your providing a session summary would be contrary to the principle of active learning.

2. Divide participants into subgroups of two to four members.

3. Ask each subgroup to create its own summary of the training session. Encourage the subgroups to create an outline, a mindmap, or any other device that will enable them to communicate the summary to others.

4. Use any of the following questions to guide the participants:

   - What were the major topics we examined?

   - What have been some of the key points raised in today's session?

   - What experiences have you had today? What did you get out of them?

   - What ideas and suggestions are you taking away from this training?

5. Invite the subgroups to share their summaries. Applaud their efforts.

Variations

1. Provide a topical outline of the day and ask participants to fill in the details of what was covered.

2. Ask participants to set the recap to music. Have them use the melody of a well-known song or let them create a musical "rap."

Case Example

In a training program on productive-group skills, members of a group summarize in their own words the following key points that contribute to group effectiveness:

- people listen and respond to one another
- the group is clear about its goals
- everyone participates
- leadership emerges from the group and is shared by all group members
- no important decision is made without making sure that everyone consents to it
- dissenting opinions are encouraged
- the well-being of the members is not ignored in favor of accomplishing the task
- the group discusses how it is doing and members give feedback to one another

Self-Assessment

The end of a training session or program is a time for reflection. What have I learned? What do I now believe? What are my skills? What do I need to improve? Allowing time for self-assessment gives participants the opportunity to examine what the training has meant to them. The strategies that follow are structured ways to promote this kind of self-assessment. They also provide a meaningful closure to the training session or program.

86 Reconsidering

Overview

One of the most effective ways to design a training session is to ask participants to state their views about the training topic right at the beginning and then to reassess these views at the end. There are several ways to accomplish this reconsideration.

Procedure

1. At the beginning of a training session, ask participants to express their views about the training topic. For example, you might ask about the following:

   - traits of an effective manager (salesperson, leader, etc.)
   - the best ways to handle employee discipline (run a meeting, etc.)
   - advice participants would give themselves to decrease stress (be more productive, be more positive, etc.)
   - solutions participants could devise for dealing with a specific problem

   Use any one of the following formats:

   - a group discussion
   - a questionnaire
   - an opening debate
   - a written statement

2. At the end of the training session, ask participants to express their views once again.

3. Ask participants whether or not their views have remained the same.

Variations

1. Discuss the reasons why participants may have changed their viewpoints.

2. Begin the session with an activity in which participants write down recent events when they were not as effective as they would have liked to be. End the session with an activity in which participants ask themselves how they would handle these events more effectively in the future.

Case Example

At the beginning of a customer-service training program, the trainer asks the participants to form subgroups and charges them with developing a list of guidelines for new customer-service representatives. The initial list includes items such as the following:

- Provide prompt service.
- Do not eat or chew gum in front of customers.
- Do not talk on the telephone while helping a customer.
- Smile.
- Refer irate customers to the manager.
- Adhere to company policy.

At the end of the training session, the trainer displays the initial list and asks participants to produce a new, improved list. The following list is generated:

- Tell the customer what you can do, not what you cannot do.
- Whenever possible, give the customer a choice.
- Put yourself in the customer's shoes.
- Go the extra mile.
- Use the customer's name.
- Try to solve the problem yourself.
- Acknowledge the customer immediately.

87 Return on Your Investment

Overview

This approach asks participants to assess whether they have profited from the training session.

Procedure

1. At the beginning of a training session, ask participants to write down how they hope to be able to use the training in their own jobs or lives. The following are some ways to structure this activity:

    - Ask participants to list their own learning goals for the session.

    - Ask participants to list recent successes and failures.

    - Ask participants to list ongoing problems, assignments, or issues at work.

2. Periodically set aside some time during the session to allow participants to read their initial statements and consider what value the training has had for them thus far.

3. At the end of the session, ask participants to assess whether their investment of time and effort in the training has been worthwhile in light of their initial comments.

4. Obtain feedback on the value of your training session from the participants.

Variations

1. Create a visual display of participants' goals so that participants can refer to them easily throughout the session.

2. Ask participants to assign a percentage to the return on their investment (ROI) in the training. For example, a participant who felt the training was helpful might indicate that she received a 75 percent return on her investment. (Sounds pretty good!)

Case Example

In a training program on presentation skills, participants are asked to list ways they could improve their presentations. A combined list is displayed:

- allay nerves at the beginning
- use presentation media more effectively
- maintain better eye contact with audience
- rely less on notes
- improve pacing
- begin with a "bang"
- avoid speaking in a monotone
- stimulate discussion and questions
- end with a strong conclusion

At the end of the program, participants are asked to assess the improvements they have made to determine the return on their investment.

88 Gallery of Learning

---**Overview**---

This activity is a way to assess and celebrate what participants have learned in a training session.

Procedure

1. Divide participants into subgroups of two to four members.

2. Ask each subgroup to discuss what it is taking away from the training session. The discussion can cover both personal and professional outcomes. Then ask the subgroups to list the "learnings" on flip-chart paper. Request that they title the list "What We Are Taking Away."

3. Paper the walls with these lists.

4. Ask participants to walk by each list and to place a check next to learnings on lists other than their own that they are taking away as well.

5. Survey the results, noting the most popular learnings. Also mention some that are unusual and unexpected.

Variations

1. If the size of the group allows, ask each participant to make his or her own list.

2. Instead of listing learnings, ask participants to list "keepers." Keepers are ideas or suggestions given in the training session that participants think are worth keeping or retaining for future use in their jobs.

Case Example

At the end of a session on motivating employees, the trainer asks each sub-group to list on flip-chart paper what it is taking away from the session. Lists include the following items:

- You cannot motivate anyone; you can only create an environment in which people are motivated from within.
- People are motivated by unmet needs.
- Rewards must be valued by the employee.
- Catch people doing something right.
- Employees will meet your expectations—either positive or negative.
- Choice and the personal commitment that results are essential to motivation.
- Reinforcement is personal. What motivates one person may not motivate another.
- Demonstrate your own motivation through behavior and attitude.
- Productivity is highest in organizations that encourage openness and trust.

89 Physical Self-Assessment

```
┌──────────────────── Overview ────────────────────┐
│                                                   │
│  This activity is similar to strategy 66, "Active Self- │
│  Assessment." Using it at the end of a training program │
│  allows participants to assess how much they have learned │
│  or to modify previously held beliefs.            │
│                                                   │
└───────────────────────────────────────────────────┘
```

Procedure

1. Create one or more statements that assess participant change. Examples might include the following:

   - I have changed my views about _____ because of this training session.

   - I have improved my skill(s) in _____.

   - I have learned new information and concepts.

2. Ask the participants to stand in the back of the room, clearing away the chairs or desks to one side.

3. Create a rating scale of numbers one through five in the front of the room by using the blackboard or by posting numbers on the wall.

4. Explain that a series of statements will be read aloud and that, after hearing each one, each participant should stand in front of the rating number that best matches his or her self-assessment. Use the following scale:

   1 = strongly disagree
   2 = disagree
   3 = not sure
   4 = agree
   5 = strongly agree

5. As each statement is read, participants should move to stand near the number that best matches their self-assessment. **Encourage participants to assess themselves realistically.** Point out that several factors might lead to little or no change. They include previous knowledge or skills or the need for more practice or time.

6. After lines form in front of the various positions, invite some participants to share why they have chosen that rating. Underscore their honesty.

7. After hearing the opinions of others, invite anyone who wishes to alter his or her position on the scale to do so.

Variations

1. Utilize a private paper-and-pencil self-assessment instead of creating a public activity.

2. Ask participants to line up in order of how much they agree with each statement. This technique, called a "physical continuum," forces participants to discuss with one another what they have learned or how they have changed as they jockey for their preferred position on the continuum.

Case Example

At the end of a session on telephone skills, the trainer prepares the following statements and shows them one at a time to the group:

- I have learned new information about how to deal with irate customers.
- I have changed my views about the importance of how I answer the telephone.
- I have improved my listening skills.
- I have learned better ways of phrasing negative statements.
- I understand that the telephone is not an interruption but an important part of my job.
- I know the appropriate procedure for transferring a call.

Participants are asked to assess themselves according to the directions in this activitiy.

90 Assessment Collage

```
┌─────────────────── Overview ───────────────────┐
│                                                 │
│  This method uses the activity of making a      │
│  picture collage to enable participants to      │
│  assess themselves in an enjoyable way.         │
│                                                 │
└─────────────────────────────────────────────────┘
```

Procedure

1. Gather several magazines. Have scissors, marking pens, and glue (or cellophane tape) available for participants.

2. Ask participants to create collages that represent what they have learned and/or how they have changed in the training program.

3. Make the following suggestions:

   - Cut out words from magazine advertisements that describe your current views, skills, or knowledge.

   - Paste on visual images that illustrate your accomplishments.

   - Use marking pens to title the collage and to add your own words or images.

4. Create a gallery of the assessment collages. Invite participants to tour the results and comment on the collages displayed.

Variations

1. Create team collages instead of individual ones.

2. Instead of a collage, have each participant create a "shield" or "crest of arms" that displays his or her accomplishments.

Case Example

For a session on professional image, the instructor explains to the participants that they now have the opportunity to create collages of pictures and words to illustrate what they have learned. The instructor distributes magazines, scissors, markers, and glue. The participants are asked to put a title on each collage. Some of the titles include the following:

- *Be All That You Can Be*
- *The First Five Seconds*
- *Dress for Success*
- *Perception Is Reality*

The following are some of the pictures and words that participants use:

Pictures

- women in suits
- a leather briefcase
- a man's trench coat
- a man's blazer
- a business card
- men in suits
- a woman in dress slacks and a blouse
- a gold watch
- a woman's skirt, blouse, and jacket ensemble
- a person smiling

Words and Phrases

- less is more
- well-groomed
- social savvy
- coordinated
- flattering
- subtle
- credibility
- confident
- right for the culture
- understated

APPLICATION PLANNING

At the conclusion of any training program, participants will naturally ask "Now what?" The success of any active training is measured by how that question is answered, that is, how what has been learned in the course is transferred back on the job. The strategies that follow are designed to promote application planning. Some are fairly quick techniques you can use when time is limited. Others require more time and commitment but lead to even better results.

91 Self-Monitoring

Overview

This strategy enables participants to develop a concrete plan to monitor themselves back on the job.

Procedure

1. Point out that a well-known technique in behavior modification is to request that the client monitor his or her own behavior. For example, in a weight loss program, a client might be asked to write down everything he or she eats on the assumption that increased awareness will bring greater self-control.

2. Suggest to participants that they closely monitor their own behavior when they return to work as a way to make training benefits last.

3. Indicate that one way to do this is for each participant to design action plans that apply what he or she has learned.

4. Have participants brainstorm "reminders" for use back on the job. Use the sentence stem "Remember to...."

5. Then ask each participant to select reminders from the brainstormed list that he or she feels are suitable for his or her job.

Variations

1. Prepare, in advance, a list of reminders for the participants. Ask them to check those they feel would be suitable.

2. Have participants make personalized "reminder" cards that they can place on their desks or hang in their worksites. Provide blank index cards and marking pens to help make the cards attractive.

Case Example

In a session on time management, the trainer asks the participants to brainstorm reminders to help them manage their time more effectively while at work. Using the sentence stem "Remember to...," the participants come up with the following reminders:

Remember to...

- make a "To Do" list every day.
- make an appointment with myself to complete a specific task.
- jot down notes and ideas on index cards.
- set priorities based on importance, not urgency.
- create a "To Read" file and carry it with me when I travel.
- skim books and articles quickly, looking for ideas.
- answer most letters and memos right on the item itself.
- delegate everything I possibly can.
- consult my list of lifetime goals once a month and revise it if necessary.
- save up trivial matters for a three-hour session once a month.

Each participant is asked to select three reminders that he or she feels have the most relevance and to place them on a card to be posted in his or her workspace.

92 Peer Consultation

┌─────────────────── **Overview** ───────────────────┐

This strategy enables participants to help one another
with on-the-job problems and, at the same time, to review and apply what they have learned in the training
program.

└──┘

Procedure

1. Form participants into subgroups for the purpose of discussing a specific
   "back on the job" issue for each participant.

2. Request that one person in each subgroup volunteer a problem he or
   she faces that is related to the training topic. Problems might include
   the following:

   ■ a difficult project

   ■ a performance review with a troubled employee

   ■ a time-management problem

   ■ a critical sales presentation

3. Ask the other members of the subgroup to help the volunteer with his or
   her problem. Urge participants to apply the knowledge and skills they
   have gained in the training program when helping the volunteer.

4. Invite each subgroup to work on as many problems as time allows.

Variations

1. Invite a participant to present a problem to the entire group. Facilitate a
   discussion so that several participants apply the knowledge and skills
   they have obtained and are able to try out their new expertise.

2. Arrange follow-up support and consultation for participants who are
   seeking help.

Case Example

Near the end of a session on meeting management, the trainer forms participants into subgroups of four and asks them to discuss upcoming meetings that they would like to manage more effectively. Each person takes a turn describing a particular aspect of the meetings that he or she would like to handle better while the other subgroup members offer input and suggestions based on learnings from the session.

One member describes a meeting in which a person tends to dominate the group. His peers suggest the following strategies:

- Tell the dominating person, in private, that he or she has a lot of good ideas but that you are concerned about the participation level of other members.

- Give the dominating person the task of recording the group's ideas.

- Use round-robin brainstorming techniques to equalize participation.

93 Obstacle Assessment

> **— Overview —**
>
> Application planning should include an assessment of those factors that might interfere with one's ability to carry out action ideas. This strategy enables participants to think about the obstacles they might face in applying what they have learned in a training program.

Procedure

1. Explain to participants your hope that they will apply the skills they have learned. Note that the best of intentions to act differently in the future can be abandoned as easily as New Year's resolutions. Indicate that this activity is designed to deal with this reality.

2. Ask participants to predict the obstacles they will have to overcome in applying what they have learned. Have them think about the circumstances that could lead to their first moment of faltering, a moment when they will revert to previously effective ways of handling a situation or fail to follow through on their resolve to undertake a plan of action. Encourage participants to visualize the scene in detail. (See strategy 57, "Imagine" for ideas to turn this reflection into a mental-imagery activity.)

3. Then guide participants in developing positive images of coping with the obstacles they may face.

4. Express confidence that participants will be able to access these positive images if the predicted negative scenarios actually unfold.

Variations

1. Instead of using mental imagery, simply ask participants to make a list of obstacles they might face. Suggest that they separate their lists into two headings: "internal" and "external." Internal obstacles refer to attitudes and actions for which participants are personally responsible. External

obstacles refer to attitudes and actions created by other people and events that interfere with one's own resolve. Ask participants to brainstorm ways to overcome these internal and external obstacles.

2. If you are familiar with it, use force-field analysis to help participants assess and overcome obstacles.[1]

Case Example

In a session on interpersonal communication, the trainer asks participants to apply what they have learned in the session back on the job. As part of action planning, the participants are asked to imagine what obstacles they might face in trying to implement their plans. One participant is planning how to give feedback to her boss about the way in which the boss criticizes her in front of coworkers. The participant visualizes approaching the boss with the following script in mind:

> *I think that I can understand that my work does not always meet your high expectations, but when you correct me in front of others, I feel embarrassed and angry. I would prefer that you talk to me privately about my performance. If you do, I will be much more receptive to your suggestions. I am concerned because I enjoy my job and want to do well and meet your expectations.*

The participant explains that she is afraid she will lose her nerve and will not speak up as she just imagined. The trainer asks her to visualize her success and her manager's positive reaction to the feedback. As an alternative, the trainer suggests that the participant write a letter instead of confronting her boss face-to-face.

---

[1] Force-field analysis is discussed on pages 144-147 in my book, *Active Training.*

94 Bumper Stickers

Overview

This strategy enables participants to create their own job aids. These may be signs or lists that are placed in or near the work area to remind participants of specific actions to take.

Procedure

1. Invite participants to create "bumper stickers" that advertise the following:

   - one thing they have learned in the training session ("Every displeased customer is a lost customer.")

   - a key thought or piece of advice they will keep in mind to guide them in the future ("Manage your emotions.")

   - an action step they will take in the future ("Ask questions when you are faced with a conflict.")

   - a question to ponder ("What is my goal?")

2. Urge participants to express themselves as concisely as possible. Have them brainstorm possibilities before making their selections. Encourage them to obtain reactions to their ideas from others.

3. Provide materials and supplies so that the participants can make the bumper stickers as attractive as possible.

4. Make a gallery display of the stickers. Make sure participants take their stickers with them to display in their work areas.

Variations

1. Provide participants with stickers made by you to take with them.

This activity is based on "Job Aids and Reminders," from *Making Training Stick* (Creative Training Techniques International, Inc.) by Dora Johnson and Barbara Carnes.

2. Have participants come up with bumper sticker ideas on index cards. Gather the cards and pass them around the group. Have each participant select three ideas from other members of the group that will serve him or her well.

Case Example

At the end of a stress management session, the trainer asks participants to create imaginary bumper stickers that capture key learning points. The participants develop the following phrases:

95 I Hereby Resolve

```
┌─────────────────── Overview ───────────────────┐
│                                                 │
│  This is a widely practiced strategy for gaining commit-  │
│  ment to applying what has been learned in the training   │
│  program. It is also an excellent way to help participants │
│  remember the training program long after it is over.     │
│                                                 │
└─────────────────────────────────────────────────┘
```

Procedure

1. Ask participants to tell you what they are taking away from the training program. Record their thoughts and display a composite list.

2. Provide participants with a blank sheet of paper and an envelope.

3. Invite the participants to write themselves a letter indicating what they (personally) are taking away from the training and what steps they intend to take to apply what they have learned. Suggest that they could begin the letter with the words "I hereby resolve...."

4. Inform the participants that the letters are confidential. Ask each participant to place his or her letter in a self-addressed envelope and to seal the envelope.

5. Ask each participant to place a Post-it™ note on the envelope with the date on which he or she wants you to mail the letter. Promise to send the letters to the participants on the dates specified.

Variations

1. Instead of having the participants write to themselves, suggest that they write to someone else, indicating their resolve and asking for support.

2. One month after the last session, send a letter to participants with a summary of the main points of the training program. Encourage them to apply what they have learned. Offer yourself as a resource in dealing with application problems.

Case Example ———————————————————————

At the end of a facilitation skills workshop, the trainer asks participants to write a letter to themselves indicating what they have learned about facilitating team meetings and how they are going to apply their learnings. The following is one participant's letter:

> *I hereby resolve to be less directive in conducting team meetings. I will ask open-ended questions and allow team members to give complete answers without interrupting them. If no one answers immediately, I will be patient and not jump in to fill the void created by silence. I will avoid giving my opinion immediately. When asked a question, I will direct it back to the team members to answer before I respond. I will make a real effort to facilitate group interaction rather than to control the meeting.*

96 Follow-up Questionnaire

Overview

This is a clever strategy for raising participants' consciousness about the training program long after it is over. It also serves as a way to stay in touch with participants.

Procedure

1. Explain to participants that you would like to send them a follow-up questionnaire one month from now. The questionnaire is intended (1) to help them assess what they have learned and how well they are doing in applying the training and (2) to give you feedback.

2. Urge the participants to fill out the questionnaire for their own benefit. Ask them to return the questionnaire only if they so desire.

3. When you develop the questionnaire, consider the following suggestions:

   - Keep the tone informal and friendly.

   - Arrange the questions so that the easiest to fill out come first. Use formats such as checklists, rating scales, incomplete sentences, and short essays.

   - Ask about what participants remember the most, what skills they are currently using, and what success they have had.

   - Offer participants the opportunity to call you with questions and application problems.

Variations

1. Send follow-up handouts that might be of interest to participants.

2. Instead of sending a questionnaire, interview participants by phone or in person. Use a small sample if the training group is large.

This activity is based on "Questionnaire," from *Making Training Stick* (Creative Training Techniques International, Inc.) by Dora Johnson and Barbara Carnes.

Case Example

After participating in a training program on assertive communication, participants are sent the following questionnaire:

Hello! How are things going? I hope you have had the opportunity to work on your assertive-communication skills. As I promised, I'm sending you this questionnaire to help you review and assess your ability to assert yourself to obtain the goals you are seeking. By sending this questionnaire back to me, you will also help me to evaluate the impact of the training program. Thanks!

1. Please rank the situations below in order of difficulty. Use a scale from 1 to 5 with 1 being the least difficult and 5 being the most difficult.

    _____ saying "no" without apologizing

    _____ initiating a conversation

    _____ stating my feelings honestly

    _____ being persuasive

    _____ handling very difficult people

2. Indicate the degree of difficulty you have in the following situations:

	No difficulty	Some difficulty	Much difficulty
talking with the opposite sex	_____	_____	_____
disciplining children	_____	_____	_____
talking on the telephone	_____	_____	_____
asking for a raise	_____	_____	_____
talking in a group	_____	_____	_____
resisting salespeople	_____	_____	_____
returning food in a restaurant	_____	_____	_____

3. Briefly describe a recent situation in which you acted assertively:

_____

_____

_____

_____

_____

_____

4. Describe a recent situation in which you did not act assertively and regretted it:

_____

_____

_____

_____

_____

5. Please circle the techniques below that you have found useful:

fogging   the broken record technique

free information   empathic assertion

"I" messages   negative inquiry

6. Check one of the following statements:

_____ Please call me. I'm having difficulty with

_____

_____

_____

_____ Everything is going well. There is no need to contact me.

———————————————

97 Sticking to It

Overview

This is a procedure in which participants make a serious commitment to apply what they have learned. The key is to combine participant action planning and supervisory feedback.

Procedure

1. At the end of the program, ask participants to fill out a follow-up form containing statements as to how they plan to implement the training. A sample form is provided on the next page.

2. When the forms are completed, tell the participants that their work statements will be sent to them in three to four weeks. At that time, also send to the participants these follow-up instructions:

   Please review your work statement follow-up form. Place the letter A next to those plans you have been able to apply successfully. Place the letter B next to those plans you are still working on applying. Place the letter C next to those plans you have not been able to apply. Explain what obstacles you have encountered that have prevented you from accomplishing your plans.

3. At each participant's discretion, you may send the work statement to his or her supervisor for feedback. The following is an example of what you might send to a supervisor:

   Supervisor's Follow-Up Note

   [Name] was a participant in a training program dealing with [subject]. During the last three to four weeks, he or she has attempted to implement the ideas or skills in the program. Please review what he or she has written. Did you observe any change? Were you able to offer your support to this person as he or she attempted to implement actions?

This activity is based on a recommendation by Sandra Merwin.

Work Statement Follow-Up Form

Describe situations in which you plan to apply material learned in this course and tell when and how you plan to apply it. Be specific.

1. Situation: _____

    _____

    My plan: _____

    _____

2. Situation: _____

    _____

    My plan: _____

    _____

3. Situation: _____

    _____

    My plan: _____

    _____

4. Situation: _____

    _____

    My plan: _____

    _____

Variations

1. Have participants share their work statements immediately with their supervisors. Suggest that the participants and their supervisors work together on a plan to help the participant "stick to it."

2. Enlist the supervisors' support of this application plan **before** the training program begins.

Case Example

A participant in a conflict-management course offers the following action plan:

1. Situation: Two employees don't get along and often have conflicts.

    My plan: Call both employees into my office and apply Fisher's suggestion to focus on "interests" rather than "positions."

2. Situation: My department and another department are competing for the same administrative support resources.

    My plan: Sit down with the manager of the other department and ask him how we can share resources in order to service the customer better.

FINAL SENTIMENTS ─────────────

In many training programs, participants develop feelings of closeness toward other group members during the sessions. This is especially true if the participants have met for a long period of time and have taken part in extensive group work. They need to say "goodbye" to one another and to express their appreciation for the support and encouragement given one another during the training program. There are many ways to help facilitate these final sentiments. The strategies that follow are some good ones.

98 Goodbye Scrabble

```
┌─────────────────── Overview ───────────────────┐
│                                                 │
│  This is a technique that enables participants to join  │
│  together at the end of a training program and celebrate │
│  what they have experienced as a group. This is achieved │
│  by creating a giant Scrabble board.            │
│                                                 │
└─────────────────────────────────────────────────┘
```

Procedure

1. Create a large display of the title of the course or training program. Merge the words in the title if there are more than one. For example, "managing change" becomes managingchange.

2. Give participants marking pens. Explain, if necessary, how words can be created using the displayed title as a base. Review the ways in which words can be listed:

   - horizontally or vertically

   - beginning with, ending with, and incorporating any available letters

   Remind participants, however, that two words cannot merge with each other—there must be a space between them. Permit proper names as words.

3. Set a time limit and invite participants to create as many key words as they can **that are associated with the content, activities, or participants in the program.**

4. Suggest that group members divide up the labor so that some participants are recording while others are searching for new words.

5. Call time and have the participants count up the words and applaud the stunning visual record of their experience with one another!

Variations

1. If the group size is unwieldy for this activity, divide the participants into subgroups and ask each subgroup to create a Scrabble board. Display all

the subgroups' results and ascertain the **total** number of words so that the session does not end on a competitive note.

2. Simplify the activity by writing the course title vertically and asking participants to write horizontally a verb, adjective, or noun that they associate with the course that begins with each letter in the title.

Case Example

An instructor for a course on delegation skills writes the word D-E-L-E-G-A-T-E vertically on a flip chart and asks participants to write words or phrases they associate with delegating that begin with the appropriate letter. The participants respond as follows:

D—do, directions, deadline
E—explain
L—listen to concerns, let go
E—encourage
G—grooms successor, gives opportunities, gives overview
A—authority, accountability, agreement
T—train (if necessary)
E—expect the best

yarn

99 Connections

Overview

This is an activity that symbolically draws a training program to a close. It is especially appropriate when participants have formed close connections with one another.

Procedure

1. Use a skein of yard to literally and symbolically connect participants.

2. Ask everyone to stand and form a circle. Start the process by stating briefly what you have experienced as a result of facilitating the training program.

3. Holding on to the end of the yarn, toss the skein to a participant on the other side of the circle. Ask that person to state briefly what he or she has experienced as a result of participating in the training program. Then ask that person to hold on to the yarn and toss the skein to another participant.

4. Have each participant take a turn at receiving the skein, sharing reflections, and tossing the yarn on, continuing to hold on to his or her segment of the yarn. The resulting visual is a web of yarn connecting every member of the group.

5. Complete the activity by stating that the program began with a collection of individuals willing to connect and learn from one another.

6. Cut the yarn with scissors so that each person, though departing as an individual, takes a piece of the other participants with him or her. Thank participants for their interest, ideas, time, and effort.

Variations

1. Ask each participant to express appreciation to the person who tossed the yarn to him or her.

2. Instead of using yarn, toss a ball or a similar object. As each person receives the ball, he or she can express final sentiments.

Case Example

As each participant in a program on secretarial cooperation receives the yarn, the following comments are made:

- I learned how important it is to work together as a team.
- I realize that we all have different personalities and communication styles.
- I appreciate being given the opportunity to get to know people on a personal level.
- I feel that I can be open and honest with everyone here.
- I now know how to deal more effectively with conflict.
- I had fun while we were learning.
- I'm going to think of ideas to streamline how we handle registration.
- You all have been a great group!

100 Group Photo

┌─── **Overview** ───┐

This is an activity that acknowledges the contributions of every participant while at the same time celebrating the total group.

└────────────────────┘

Procedure

1. Assemble participants for a group photograph. It is best to create at least three rows of participants: one row sitting on the floor, one row sitting in chairs, and one row standing behind the chairs. As you are about to take the picture, express your own final sentiments. Stress how much active training depends on the support and involvement of participants. Thank participants for playing such a large part in the success of the program.

2. Then invite one participant at a time to leave the group and to be the photographer. (*Optional:* Have each participant merely come up and view what a final picture of the group would look like.)

3. If the group is not too large, ask each participant to share his or her final thoughts with the group. Ask the group to applaud each participant for his or her contributions to the group.

4. When the film is developed, send each participant his or her own photograph of the group.

Variations

1. Use the photography session as an opportunity to review some of the highlights of the program.

2. Instead of a public disclosure of sentiments, ask participants to write final thoughts on sheets of paper taped to the walls.

Case Example

A training program on cross-functional teams is about to end. Participants have spent many hours examining opportunities for cross-functional collaboration in their organization and have developed specific action plans for implementation. As a final activity, the trainer assembles the participants for a group photo. As each participant serves as photographer, final sentiments are expressed. Among them are the following:

- I thought this was going to be a waste of time because different units would only be interested in protecting their "turf." Was I wrong! I'm really excited about the work we've done together.

- I'm really impressed by the talent in this group. We can't miss.

- In the beginning, I wasn't sure we would ever get to the point of listening to one another. By the end, I really trusted everyone.

- Although I'm not as optimistic as many others are, I think it's worth a shot. You can count on me to be there.

101 The Final Exam

┌─────────────── **Overview** ───────────────┐

This is an enjoyable way to reminisce about activities that have taken place in a training program of at least one day's length.

└──┘

Procedure

1. Give participants a blank sheet of paper and tell them that it is time for their "final exam." Keep them in suspense about the exam.

2. Tell the participants that their task is to write down, in order, the many activities they have experienced in the training program. (At this point, reveal that this is a challenge that will not be graded.)

3. After each participant has finished (or given up!), have the full group generate a list. Make adjustments until a complete list is obtained.

4. With the list in view, ask participants to reminisce about these experiences, recalling moments of fun, cooperation, and insight.

5. Facilitate the discussion so that the exchange of memories brings a strong emotional closure to the training program.

Variations

1. Provide the list of activities. Start the reminiscing immediately.

2. Rather than focusing on activities, focus on "moments to remember." Leave this phrase open to interpretation. This may create a laughter-filled and perhaps nostalgic review of the training program.

Case Example ─────────────────────────────────

Participants in a training program on creativity have experienced a day filled with activities that promote novel thinking. The participants are given newsprint and asked to recall the activities using a "mindmapping" process (one of the techniques they have learned). The result looks like the following:

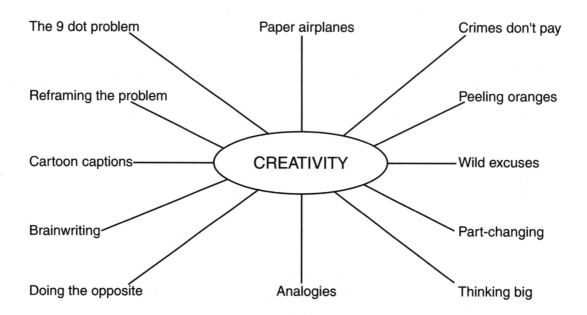

When the participants finish, the trainer asks them to reminisce about these activities, recalling moments of fun, cooperation, and insight.

INDEX TO CASE EXAMPLES

About the Authors

Dr. Mel Silberman is a professor of adult and organizational development at Temple University, where he specializes in adult training and development. He has conducted numerous active-training seminars for educational, corporate, government, and human-service organizations world wide. He is also president of Active Training in Princeton, New Jersey, a firm specializing in instructional-skills development. Dr. Silberman can be contacted by telephone at 609-924-8157.

Dr. Silberman has authored or edited many books, including *Active Training: A Handbook of Techniques, Designs, Case Examples, and Tips* (Lexington Books, 1990), *20 Active Training Programs, Vol. I* (Pfeiffer & Company, 1992), and *20 Active Training Programs, Vol. II* (Pfeiffer & Company, 1994).

Dr. Silberman is a graduate of Brandeis University and holds an M.A. and a Ph.D. in educational psychology from the University of Chicago.

Karen Lawson is president of Lawson Consulting Group, an organization and management-development consultant firm in Lansdale, Pennsylvania. She has over twenty years of experience in the fields of management, training, consulting, and education across a wide range of industries. Ms. Lawson is director of the National ASTD Sales and Marketing Professional Practice Area and was president of the Philadelphia/Delaware Valley Chapter of ASTD and the Liberty Bell Chapter of the National Speakers Association. Ms. Lawson was an editor of and contributor to *20 Active Training Programs, Vol. II.*

Editor: Susan Rachmeler
Production Editor: Dawn Kilgore
Cover Design: Susan Odelson
Interior Design and Page Composition: Judy Whalen
Illustrations: Lee Ann Hubbard

This book was edited and formatted using 486 platforms with 8MB RAM and high-resolution, dual-page monitors. The copy was produced using Word-Perfect software; pages composed with Corel Ventura software; illustrations produced in Corel Draw. The text is set in thirteen on fifteen New Baskerville and heads are Stone Serif Bold and Bold Italic.